Work Songs

Matt Johnson

The Impossible Company
Richmond
2020

Copyright © 2020 by Matt Johnson

All rights reserved. No part of this publication may be reproduced, stored in a retrieval system, or transmitted in any form or by any means—electronic, mechanical, photocopy, recording, or any other—except for brief quotations in printed reviews, without the prior permission of the publisher.

Although every precaution has been taken to verify the accuracy of the information contained herein, the author and publisher assume no responsibility for any errors or omissions. No liability is assumed for damages that may result from the use of the information contained within.

These words are the author's own and do not represent any government, company, or outside cause.

Published in the United States by
The Impossible Company, Richmond.

The Impossible Company Hardcover ISBN: 978-0-9962888-2-8
eBook ISBN: 978-0-9962888-3-5

COVER ART BY *Max Kuhn* AND LAYOUT BY *Brad Clifford*
INTERIOR DESIGN BY *Madison Johnson*
EDITING BY *Katherine Schutt*

Printed in the United States of America
10 9 8 7 6 5 4 3 2 1

To the songs that made us who we are.

CONTENTS

Introduction vi

I: Origin Stories 3

II: The Struggle 25

III: Human Things 43

IV: Meaning 65

V: Legacy 83

Conclusion 102

Acknowledgements 104

INTRODUCTION

ALAN LOMAX BELIEVED THAT NO SONG should ever die. He probably got this notion from his dad, who was a professor and celebrated authority on Texas folklore and cowboy songs. Through his research, Lomax's father was alarmed to find that more and more of America's oldest songs were not being picked up by younger generations. And since most of these field, folk, and sea songs had never been recorded, many were at risk of disappearing forever.

Lomax couldn't accept this. So he spent 60 years as an ethnomusicologist on a mission to record the endangered songs of the world. A mission that brought him and his partner, Shirley Collins, to the Mississippi State Penitentiary on a warm day in mid-September 1959. They were there to record the work songs of the Southern prison farms. The guards led Lomax and Collins out to a field where a group of inmates were chopping wood.

After Lomax set up his stereo recorder, James Carter and his fellow inmates started singing a song called, "Po' Lazarus." It's a bluesy old work song about a man who is gunned down by a sheriff with a .44. There were no instruments, just the synchronized sounds of the axes hitting a log. The song was eventually released on a record called *Bad Man Ballads* as part of Lomax's 1960 *Southern Journey* LP Series on Prestige International Records.

And there it would stay until the year 2000. That's when a music producer named T Bone Burnett remembered hearing the song years before, and he added it to the soundtrack for a new Coen Brothers movie called *O Brother, Where Art Thou?* The movie was a success, but the soundtrack was even bigger. It would go on to win three Grammy Awards and sell more than four million copies.

But whatever happened to the men who sang its first song?

Alan Lomax's daughter, Anna, did not feel right keeping the royalties for a song that her father didn't sing. So, she searched the archives of the Mississippi penal system, Social Security files, and property records to eventually discover that James Carter was alive and living in Chicago with his wife. Anna booked a flight to deliver three things to Carter: a $20,000 royalty check, a platinum record bearing his name, and plane tickets for him and the family to attend the 2002 Grammy Awards.

Carter didn't really remember recording the song, and when Anna told him that it was selling better than Michael Jackson, he had to leave the room to roll a cigarette. When he came back, Carter smiled and said, "You tell Michael that I'll slow down so that he can catch up with me."[1] Carter went on to make over $100,000 in royalties. He bought his church a van, got a new apartment, and donated to the local food bank.[2]

One more work song saved.

For as long as we've had language, we've had songs for the work we do. Whether they are sea shanties bellowed defiantly against gale-force winds, field songs sung under blistering sun, or industrial folk tunes set to the rhythm of the machines that run, work songs helped our ancestors fight boredom, find meaning, build connections, and survive. And these songs didn't only play a critical role for the people who wrote and sang them; they also shaped music as we know it today. Just ask Sam Cooke, Bob Dylan, Aretha Franklin, Woody Guthrie, Pete Seeger, Billy Bragg, and so many more.

But modern work has no song. We sing no hymns in the offices, factories, fields, shops, and restaurants where we work today. We let the music die, and we did it when we needed it the most. As H.P. Lovecraft once said, "Toil without song is like a weary journey without an end." So, it's no wonder that so many of us feel increasingly empty and disconnected at work.

When Lomax set out to record those endangered songs, it wasn't about the music—it was about the meaning. Because each song that he recorded was a story. A story that helped people endure struggle, inspire, teach, mobilize, and redefine what's possible with the work they do. And Lomax knew that once those stories faded away, we would lose many of the generational lessons that made us who we are today. We would lose a part of ourselves.

And that's what this book is all about.

This is a collection of stories about work that we cannot let die. Whether it's the courage of journalist Nellie Bly to go undercover in a deplorable insane asylum, the emptiness of success that led to an early death for the boxer Sonny Liston, or the fight that inspired Bruce Springsteen to write the biggest hit of his life, it is my hope that the stories in this book will do what the work songs of yore did before: Help us fight boredom, find meaning, build connections, and survive.

So with that, we tip the hat to James Carter, the prisoners, and all of the others who sang the songs that shaped who we are.

Now it's time to sing ours.

Work Songs

I. ORIGIN STORIES

"I'll play it first and tell you what it is later."

—*Miles Davis*

Our Greatest Expectations

PABLO PICASSO WALKED INTO AN apartment to find Gertrude Stein sitting in a high-backed Renaissance chair with drink in hand and Henri Matisse by her side. This was Paris in March 1906. Stein was hosting one of her now-famous Saturday evening salon dinners, and none of them knew it then, but this one would change the future of art.

Matisse was an increasingly popular modern artist at the time. Known for his bold use of color, his friend André Derain once said that for Matisse, "Colors became sticks of dynamite."[3] Picasso, on the other hand, was relatively unknown. Just a few years before, he was reportedly burning his work to keep his room warm. But Stein saw something special in Picasso.[4] She bought most of his early work believing that once more people saw it, they would agree that Picasso was one of the greatest artists this world would ever see.

She was right. While Picasso and Matisse were somewhat skeptical of each other, the two did interact quite a bit that night. And during their conversation, Matisse showed Picasso a wooden figurine from what is now the Democratic Republic of the Congo that he had just bought from a curio shop nearby.[5] Picasso was transfixed. The elongated torso and upturned, mask-like face lit a spark of curiosity deep inside.

In the days that followed, Picasso went to the ethnographic museum at the Palais du Trocadéro and immersed himself in African art. The dramatic masks, totems, and carved figures moved him, and he spent the next nine months working on an eight-foot-tall painting that he called *Les Demoiselles d'Avignon*. This painting features five nude prostitutes in a brothel in Barcelona, and two of them have faces that look just like those African masks he studied. The piece would go on to become the most famous cubist painting in the world.

But this story isn't about the art; it's about those dinners.

Following in the tradition of the 18th-century Parisian salons that fueled the Enlightenment, Gertrude Stein and her brother Leo had been hosting weekly gatherings for years. There was no formal agenda; they simply brought together people whose work they admired, including James Joyce, Ezra Pound, Virginia Woolf, Ernest Hemingway, F. Scott Fitzgerald, Picasso, Matisse, and so many more. Stein would call them The Lost Generation—a collection of creators who were left disoriented and wandering in the wake of World War I.

The irony is that those lost souls would help future generations find themselves. They invented modern art, and their writing gave people new meaning in war, depression, love, betrayal, and the like. And much like the African figurine that inspired one of Picasso's greatest works, these dinners played no small part in the group's other creations. Hemingway's conversations with Stein and Sherwood Anderson led him to embrace a writing style in *The Sun Also Rises* that omits words to create meaning. F. Scott Fitzgerald's final novel, *Tender is the Night*, is filled with characters inspired by his time at those dinners. These gatherings offer us an important lesson for what and how we create.

When you expect big things to happen, they just might.

Whether it's Ginsberg and Kerouac at Kenneth Rexroth's apartment, Warhol and Dylan at the Factory, or Stein and Picasso at 27 Rue de Fleurus, salons like these changed our world. And it's not just that these people were more creative and capable than us. It's that they had a place that wasn't only about what is—it was about what could be. And that shared expectation that something big might happen is the real source of genius here.

We've known for quite some time that human expectations are powerful. In 1966, a Harvard professor named Robert Rosenthal and an elementary school principal named Lenore Jacobson published results from their now-famous study on how teacher's expectations shape student performance.[6] Specifically, they found that after teachers were told that 20 percent of their students had unusual potential for intellectual growth, those kids showed greater gains in IQ eight months later. This despite the fact that those "unusually bright" students were really just randomly selected. It was expectations, not IQ, that fueled the rise.

In the time since, many other studies have shown the power of our own expectations and those around us to shape what we believe and achieve. In her 1940 book, *Paris France*, Stein wrote, "One of the pleasant things those of us who write or paint do is to have the daily miracle. It does come." And that's what those salons were all about. So, when Picasso walked into Stein's apartment that spring night in 1906, he likely didn't just expect to do some drinking or networking with fellow artists;

he came prepared for his world to change. And that's probably why it did.

Most of us don't have a place where we believe that big things will happen. It's not part of our social fabric or modern work. We have meetings, happy hours, play dates, sports games, date nights, concerts, camping trips, and the like, but maybe there's room for one more thing. A night where we gather not to talk about what is, but what could be.

A night defined by our greatest expectations.

The Impossible Dreams

IN 1961, A SMALL GROUP OF MEN WAS living on the side of a mountain in Saudi Arabia. They were there to build a road that would shape the future of the kingdom. The Al-Sarawat mountain range extended 1,000 miles along the Red Sea from the border with Jordan all the way to Yemen, effectively dividing the country in two. And the terrain along the range was so rugged that no previous generation was able to build a road through. Commerce and progress would have to wait.

But Faisal bin Abdulaziz wanted to change that. When he became king, he offered an exorbitant sum of money to the first construction firm that could build a road from Mecca to the Red Sea. Companies flocked in from all over the world to survey the land, but not one would submit a bid. Why?

Because even if you could blast through the tons of hard granite, no one knew how to get excavators, bulldozers, backhoes, and graders to the site.

The king was defeated.

But one day, a small local firm offered to build the road in less than two years for a modest budget. While the king had his doubts, he also had no other option. He granted the contract, and the men packed up to go to live on the side of a mountain for the next 16 months.

The first thing they did was follow a donkey up and over the range to mark the path of least resistance. This would be their road. After blasting the path, they came up against the intractable challenge of getting the equipment to the site. Their answer? Disassemble the large earthmovers and graders, put the pieces on the backs of donkeys and camels, walk a caravan to the site, unload and reassemble the equipment, and then build that road.[7] And that's exactly what they did. A kingdom united.

What was it that enabled this small, inexperienced company to do the thing that no multimillion-dollar firm could? Story. The story that fueled those large firms was all about minimizing risk and maximizing profit. And if you're only thinking about risk and profit, you won't walk with that caravan up the mountain. You won't give the blood it takes to bring dreams to life.

But for that local firm, the story was about the future of the country. They knew the shop owners who would gain access to global markets, the people who would benefit from increased oil revenue, and the countless other lives that would change. Nothing would stop them from building that road.

That's why story is the most powerful human invention. This is not hyperbole. Story is the reason that we, as a species, rose from mid-level primates to the rulers of the world.

The first couple million years of human existence were really just a prehistoric groundhog day: ape-like hominids living in small groups struggling to survive against the threat of starvation, cave bears, wolves, eagles, saber-toothed cats, and even giant kangaroos. But, as Yuval Harari outlined in his book, *Sapiens*, roughly 70,000 years ago everything changed. We discovered fire, and this enabled us to cook nutritious food that would eventually bring our brains to life. It was a cognitive revolution that had us thinking new big thoughts and creating language to communicate them.[8] This was our defining moment, because unlike all other animals that use communication to describe reality, we were now able to create it.

What fueled our rise exactly? Human cooperation. No other animal species can cooperate in large numbers, but the stories we tell can mobilize collective action at scale. We didn't spontaneously land on the moon, build great pyramids, or eradicate smallpox. All great human achievements were born from the stories that propelled cooperation.

Our great challenge now is to keep up with the world that storytelling created. A world inundated with narratives designed to distract—and often divide—us. Narratives fraying the social fabric of our countries, communities, and families, while also diverting our attention away from our own ambitions and collective vision.

Of course, this is not the first time that a great human virtue evolved to become a vice. In their 1968 book, *The Lessons of History*, Ariel and Will Durant observed that "Probably every vice was once a virtue ... Man's sins may be the relics of his rise rather than the stigmata of his fall." And so we stand at an inflection point between the virtue and vice of the story we'll write, facing the question of a generation.

Do we still believe in the impossible dreams?

The White Whale and Rituals We Lost

IN 1853, THE NEW YORK CITY warehouse for the publishing company Harper and Brothers burst into flames. The fire started after a plumber lit a lamp with a roll of paper and then tried to extinguish it in a tub of what he thought was water. Unfortunately, the tub contained a chemical called camphine, used to clean ink from the rollers; within seconds, the building was ablaze. All of the employees safely evacuated, but thousands of books burned.[9]

Many of the books were reprinted, but one title was not immediately replaced. It was a sea story about a whaling expedition gone terribly wrong. A captain named Ahab led his men on a hopeless journey to exact revenge on the white whale that took his leg. You probably know this story;

the whale's name was Moby Dick. And Herman Melville's book by the same name is now widely considered one of the greatest and most popular stories ever written.

But how did this once-unknown book become what it is today?

By the time Herman Melville published *Moby Dick* in 1851, he was already a relatively well-known author. Two of his previous books, *Typee* and *Omoo*, sold quite well with their romanticized accounts of life in the Polynesian Islands. However, despite the success of his early work, *Moby Dick* was not well received.

One review from the *London Spectator* said that the book, "repels the reader instead of attracting him."[10] It was universally panned and Melville was only able to sell 3,715 copies before it finally went out of print.[11] From there, Melville wrote a few more articles, books, and poems, but none took hold. So, in 1866 he took a job as a customs inspector for the City of New York and stayed in that role for the next 19 years.

Melville had a heart attack and died at his house in New York City on the morning of September 28, 1891. His death was not at all the global event that it would be today, and there was very little press coverage. The *New York Times* did publish an article a few days later, but it wasn't necessarily flattering, as it ended with this sentence: "The latest book, now about a quarter of a century old, *Battle Pieces and Aspects of the War*, fell flat and he has died an absolutely forgotten man."[12]

Not exactly a rousing tribute for the author of a great American novel.

It wasn't until 1919 that Melville would get his shot at redemption. A Columbia University graduate student named Raymond Weaver was at an annual spring dinner when Professor Carl Van Doren, also the editor for *The Nation*, offered him an assignment.[13] Van Doren wanted to run a short tribute to honor Melville's 100th birthday. Weaver didn't particularly want the assignment, but he needed the money.

After diving in on the project, Weaver started to see that this wasn't some obscure author from the past. He believed Melville's work was important, and he was increasingly determined to help the world see it. Weaver wrote that article for *The Nation*, and then spent the next two years writing Melville's biography.

Weaver's work gained the attention of New York's literary elite, and their collective influence helped Melville become revered as one of the greatest writers in American history. *Moby Dick* went on to sell millions of copies, and it inspired countless artists, writers, and musicians, including Ernest Hemingway, Bob Dylan, Jackson Pollock, Albert Camus, Led Zeppelin, Ray Bradbury, Jack Kerouac, Cormac McCarthy, and so many more.

But why? Musings from academics and journalists answering that very question can now fill volumes much longer than the book itself. But to the extent there is consensus, it's this: *Moby Dick* is popular because it helps us understand and endure life's biggest tragedies. As generations read about the harsh conditions of life at sea on a mission doomed to fail, they gain a new understanding of and appreciation for what it means to be alive in the face of terrifying change. Because learning about the struggles that other people endure can help us make it through our own.

This is not a new idea. The premise is one that American professor Joseph Campbell used to define his career. He popularized the idea that myths and their related rituals are the most powerful tools we have to fuel human development. It's why every society, from the Bushmen of Botswana to the Roman Empire, has had myths and rituals to help their people understand and mark the transition to adulthood, birth of a child, sacrifice in war, love of another, and every other major life change.

But with the decline of organized religion and a cohesive social identity, we now have a world where myths and rituals are no longer a central part of life's defining moments. And as Campbell once told Bill Moyers, "If you want to find out what it means to have a society without any rituals, read the *New York Times*."[14]

I used to think that fiction wasn't worth reading because the stories weren't true. But then the prehistoric remains of a previously unknown predatory whale were discovered in Peru in 2008. The massive creature was named *Livyatan melvillei* as a tribute to the man who wrote *Moby Dick*. And that's when I learned the real lesson from Melville's most famous myth. The most important stories don't document history; they help us make it.

To the myths and rituals we need the most.

The Letter That Went Around the World

IN 1885, THE *PITTSBURG DISPATCH* published an article titled "What Girls are Good For." Written by Erasmus Wilson, a journalist known as the Quiet Observer, the piece railed against the idea that women should do anything other than cooking, chores, mothering, and other related tasks inside the house.[15] As you might imagine, this received significant criticism from many in the community.

In response, one woman wrote a blistering letter back to the paper's editor and anonymously signed it as "Lonely Orphan Girl." Impressed by the writing, the editor published an ad in the Sunday paper inviting the author of the letter to come to the office for proper recognition. The next day, 20-year-old Elizabeth Cochran showed up, and the editor invited her to turn her letter into a rebuttal piece about the struggles of modern women. Cochran wrote the piece, it was well-received, and the *Dispatch* gave her a full-time writing position under the pen name Nellie Bly.[16] This was the birth of investigative journalism.

Bly hit the ground running, taking on an assignment to write an eight-part series exposing dangerous and exploitative conditions for women in many of Pittsburgh's factories. Soon after that, she took a six-month assignment in Mexico to expose political corruption from a repressive government.[17] Under threat of arrest, Bly fled back to Pittsburgh where the paper thought it best to reassign her to a fashion and gossip column on the women's page.

Bly turned down the assignment, resigned in protest, and went to New York City, where she talked her way into a meeting with Joseph Pulitzer, the editor of the *New York World* newspaper. Bly had heard about deplorable conditions at the insane asylum on Blackwell's Island between Manhattan and Queens, but no press were authorized inside. She told Pulitzer that she would have herself committed to the asylum to report on the truth.

Pulitzer loved the idea, and Bly never looked back. She practiced looking deranged in the mirror, deprived herself of sleep, then checked into a working-class boardinghouse. There, Bly launched a series of conspiratorial rants about theft from her housemates, causing such a commotion that the police were eventually called to take her away. From there, she convinced the police, a judge, and multiple doctors that she was clinically insane.

Bly was committed to Blackwell's Island in short order. Once inside, she discovered horrific conditions, including rancid butter on moldy toast, ice baths and freezing temperatures, forced sitting on straight-back benches for 14 hours a day, broom-handle beatings, excessive drug dosages, and more. It was hell, and after 10 days, Bly started to feel her sanity slip away. Lawyers from *New York World* intervened and secured her release. Two days later, on October 9, 1887, the paper released the first of a two-part exposé.

News traveled fast, and authorities started an investigation that included a grand jury visit to the facility with Bly.

The asylum's leadership had no choice but to improve living conditions, and the government added an additional $1 million—an unprecedented amount—to the asylum's budget. Bly became an overnight celebrity, and went on to do a number of different exposés, including one uncovering an underground baby trade in New York.

Next, Bly pitched another idea to Pulitzer. After reading Jules Verne's fictional story "Around the World in 80 Days," she decided that she could make the same trip in less time. Pulitzer gave her the green light. She left a few days later with one dress, underwear, a small leather bag, and a long coat. Bly traveled by railroad, boat, and burro to finish the trip in 72 days, 6 hours, 11 minutes, and 14 seconds.[18] A new world record.

Bly eventually met and married a man who ran a factory that made steel milk containers, stackable garbage cans, and boilers. When he died, she took over the company—relatively uncharted territory for women in her time. Years later, Bly would write a series of dispatches from the Eastern Front during World War I and report on the women's suffrage movement. She remained an active writer until she died of pneumonia in 1922 at age 57.

This is about the difference between the plans we make and the paths we take. Bly's life was one governed principally by spontaneity and courage. She didn't plan to write an anonymous letter that impressed the newspaper editor enough to offer her a job. She just wrote a letter that she felt compelled to write, and it changed her life.

In a world hyper-focused on productivity and achievement, it makes sense that most will ruthlessly prioritize a rational plan for success on the road ahead. But if we can learn anything from Nellie Bly, it's this: Our life-defining moments are not born from the plans we make, but the impromptu opportunities we take. And we can't focus so hard on our plans that we miss them.

Pick up your head and open your eyes.

Lost Songs and Polaroids

THERE WAS A KNOCK AT THE DOOR. Rick Rubin walked over and opened it to find an excited musician standing there. The 64-year-old man wanted to talk about some of the work they had done over a decade before. This was not unusual since Rubin possesses one of the most diverse resumes in music history, producing records for Adele, AC/DC, Kanye West, Johnny Cash, Metallica, Justin Timberlake, Slayer, and so many more.

The visitor's name was Tom Petty, and he wanted to talk about a record that never came out. From 1992 to 1994, the pair recorded more than 25 songs for an album called *Wildflowers*. Though they originally planned for it to be a double album, Warner Bros. President Larry Waronker persuaded Petty to cut it down to 15 tracks.[19] Single-length records are easier to sell, and that's exactly what *Wildflowers* did—to the tune of more than 3.2 million copies. But 10 incredible songs never saw the light of day.

And that's what Petty wanted to talk about that day. He had been thinking about the unreleased tracks and wanted Rubin to hear them again. When he did, Rubin was floored, later telling Malcom Gladwell that, "I had, like, a vague memory of them, but some of them just hit me like, 'Wow, what a great song! How did we ever miss this?'"[20] So, he asked Petty if he would like to collaborate to release the songs.

Petty said no. Though he agreed the songs were special, he knew he could not authentically present them as new since he was past the time where he could have written them. That prolific period in his career was over, and that was that. The songs would stay on the shelf until Tom Petty died on October 2, 2017.[21]

This is about the creativity that creates us.

In her second memoir, *M Train*, Patti Smith wrote about visiting Sylvia Plath's grave on two different occasions. Each time she was there, she took Polaroid pictures of the grave, which she brought home to add to large stacks from over the years. Smith treated these stacks like tarot card decks, randomly pulling Polaroids at different times to reconnect with memories gone by.

Later, Smith realized that she had somehow lost the pictures of Plath's grave. So, with her vintage Polaroid Land 250 in hand, she took a third trip there with her sister. Smith tried her best to recreate the old shots, but ended up acquiescing that the new picture, while nice, did not have the shimmering quality of the lost ones. This sequence of events led Smith to write something more profound than any Polaroid: "Nothing can be truly replicated. Not a love, not a jewel, not a single line."[22]

Many of us see the creative process as if the creator is a stationary and stable sun with their creations orbiting as planets around them. The sun remains mostly the same as its planets evolve and change. In reality, our work creates us as much as we create it, and when we are done, we are different. It's why Bob Dylan once said that he doesn't know who wrote his early records.[23]

It's also why an older Tom Petty didn't release the extra *Wildflowers* songs—he's not the man who wrote them. And why Patti Smith couldn't replicate those first two Polaroids—she's not the woman who took them. Once we see that our work makes us as much as we make it, we become aware that our greatest creation will not be the next record, book, poem, painting, or song.

It's us.

Road Trip Revelations

JOHN BURROUGHS DID NOT LIKE the Model T. In 1908, the famous nature writer who helped to spark America's conservation movement denounced the car as a "demon on wheels" that would "seek out even the most secluded nook or corner of the forest and befoul it with noise and smoke."[24] Not exactly a raving review for America's new favorite automobile.

As an avid bird watcher and Burroughs admirer, the critique cut deep for Henry Ford. To him, the automobile offered a novel way to enjoy nature, not destroy it. A way for people to explore and connect with the land he loved. So, Ford sent a letter to Burroughs explaining why he thought affordable automobiles would change the future of America.

The letter arrived with a new Model T—which Burroughs accidentally drove through the side of a barn. Still, he was persuaded by Henry Ford's vision. The two went on to exchange many more letters, and a deep friendship emerged. Ford introduced Burroughs to Thomas Edison and Harvey Firestone, and in 1914 the group decided to embark on an adventure to the Florida Everglades. It was the birth of the great American road trip.

They called themselves The Vagabonds and embarked on a camping trip each year from 1914 through 1924. They averaged 18 miles per hour, puttering their way to the Adirondacks, Catskills, Smoky Mountains, California's sparkling coast, and the maple forests of Vermont, among others. Naturally, the quartet encountered no shortage of adventure, whether picking apples for an orchard owner, helping a farmer cradle his crop of oats, or hitching a short ride on a passing train.

Ford served as the mechanic, Edison navigated (always opting for backroads), Firestone cooked the meals (usually while reciting poetry), and Burroughs led botanical hikes at each stop. They debated philosophy, economics, world war, and which sap-filled plants might be a natural alternative to rubber. But no matter how intense those debates got, they always agreed on one thing: Business should be a force for good.

Burroughs wrote about this in a travel essay in which he shared that Ford was "always thinking in terms of the greatest good to the greatest number." And that Edison started every venture by asking, "What can I do to make life easier and more enjoyable to my fellow man?"[25]

It's an idea worth revisiting today. Because we stand in the wake of one of the largest and most destructive experiments in history—the belief that companies should serve shareholders above all else.

This belief gained popularity in the 1970s, when academic economists began celebrating something they called agency theory. At the theory's core is the assertion that since shareholders own the corporation, they should have ultimate authority over all major business decisions. And that by maximizing profit for shareholders, companies would also benefit customers, employees, and society at large.

It sounds reasonable on its face, but that's not exactly how it played out. With outsourced labor, reduced investment in research and development, recurring scandals, mass layoffs, wage stagnation, environmental destruction, reduced funding for employee development, and increasing pressure to deliver short-term returns, we've seen a wave of unintended consequences from this shift to shareholder primacy.

Adding insult to injury, the shift actually hasn't generated more value for shareholders. The University of Toronto calculates that from 1932 through 1976, the total real compound annual return on the stocks of the S&P 500 was 7.6 percent, while the comparable return in the years after 1976 was just 6.4 percent.[26] Add in the fact that the average lifespan of an S&P 500 company has declined from over 60 years in the 1950s to less than 20 today, and one thing is clear: This experiment didn't work.

Don't worry, this is not a socialist manifesto. And even if it was, most of us are not in a position to shift this prevailing corporate governance model. That said, at an individual level, there is one thing that each of us can do: Always create more value than you capture.

If you consistently deliver more value than you get in return, whether to your customers, coworkers, or community, you will win. It's why media CEO Tim O'Reilly and billionaire investor Ray Dalio see it as the philosophy that guides the work they do. And Henry Ford did too. Despite some of his later moral failures, he often said, "The only true test of values, either of [people] or of things, is that of their ability to make the world a better place in which to live."

Which brings us back to The Vagabonds. Thomas Edison died at his home in Orange, New Jersey, on October 18, 1931. His son Charles was by his side, and when he saw his father start to fade away, he placed a test tube by his mouth to catch his last breath. Charles sealed the tube and delivered it to his dad's best friend, Henry Ford. It remains on display at the Ford Museum today.[27]

Even though all of The Vagabonds are gone, we still have that last breath. A permanent reminder of the legacy they left. A reminder that good work is always good for the world.

Let's never forget it again.

II. THE STRUGGLE

"I was a mailman walking in the snow six days a week."
—John Prine

Meeting in the Deep

RODNEY MULLEN WAS HANGING upside down with his hip wedged against the wheel well of a car. It was 1:30 a.m., and he had been doing this every night for the last two years as part of an elaborate plan to heal himself. After 33 years of skateboarding at the highest level, Mullen suffered from a debilitating hip injury. He could barely walk more than 50 yards at a time, let alone skate.[28]

Mullen's doctor said that his injury was similar to someone who had been in a front-end collision. The scar tissue was so thick that it was jamming his femur into his hip socket. No real cure existed, and his doctor was convinced that his skateboarding days were done. Mullen asked if there was any way to heal himself, and his doctor told him, likely in jest, that he could systematically apply pressure with a blunt object for a few thousand hours to break up the strands of fascia. That was all he needed to hear.

Mullen was no stranger to discipline. Born in 1966 in Gainesville, Florida, he started skateboarding at age 10. By the time his family moved to a farm in rural Florida a few years later, skateboarding was a daily routine. Rain or shine, Mullen spent two hours a day skating on a concrete pad outside his garage.[29] His monastic discipline fueled an unprecedented rise. Mullen won his first competition at the age of 14 and went on to finish first in 35 of 36 competitions that he entered. Today, Rodney Mullen is considered the godfather of street skateboarding.

It's a great story, but we have to be careful with it. A rural kid from modest means gives everything to his craft to become the best there ever was. This is the epitome of rags to riches, and we love it. We celebrate the rise. We admire the fame, the money, and all that comes with it. No doubt, Mullen will be the first to tell you that those things were great in the beginning. But after that, he will tell you about a story called "The Burrow."

Franz Kafka penned the tale. It features a mole-like creature that spent his life building an elaborate and impressive system of tunnels. However, as much as the creature wanted to rest to enjoy his creation, he lived in constant fear of an attack. So, he spent his days patrolling its tunnels without rest to protect them from foreign threats and destruction.

Mullen felt this tyranny of success from the time he won his first big competition in 1979. He couldn't find peace or pride in his accomplishments because he was too focused on trying to keep them. Eventually, Mullen got very depressed.

When you first encounter the emptiness of success, you have a choice. You can continue to search for higher highs, usually through drugs, money, or pleasures of the flesh (a well-worn path to oblivion), or you can redefine what success means. Mullen chose the latter, and he did it by reflecting on what truly brought him joy.

Surprisingly, his answer was not to dial back his obsessive training regimen at all. Those repetitive hours learning and inventing new maneuvers actually brought him the most joy. Competing did not. So, Mullen quit doing competitions and threw away all of his trophies. His training was no longer the means to success; it *was* success. Even though he was no longer achieving new heights, Mullen understood he was reaching new depths.

Jack Kerouac understood this too, a good 15 years before Mullen was born. In 1950, Kerouac wrote his great friend Ed White a letter. In it he said, "I want to fish as deep down as possible in my own subconscious in the belief that, once that far down, everyone will understand because they are the same that far down."[30]

And maybe that's just it. Maybe when we celebrate these rags-to-riches stories from afar, it's not the fame, money, or accolades we admire. Maybe it's that when we watch someone work so tirelessly, we don't just see their potential, we see ours. Because when they fish deep down in their subconscious, they are the same as us.

So we go back to the wheel well. It was 3:30 a.m. and Mullen had been working his hip for two hours. With a running nose and tears streaming down his face, he reached his hand around to the axel, pulled his hip into the wheel well, and...*snap*.[31] Mullen had broken many bones, but never heard a noise like this. He collapsed to the ground, and cautiously tried to stand. For the first time in years, his leg moved freely without major pain. The godfather was on his board again.

We break through by digging deep, not climbing high.

The Give and Take of the Gilded Age

LOUIS LINGG WOKE UP IN THE Cook County Jail on November 10, 1887. It would be the most important day of his life. To mark the occasion, Lingg's close friend, Dyer Lum, had dropped off a cigar as a gift. At 9 a.m. that morning, Lingg lit the cigar and blew his jaw clean off his face.[32] He fell to the ground, dipped his hand in the blood on the floor, and wrote a message in German on the wall: "Hoch die anarchie!"

Hurrah for anarchy. Lingg was set to face the gallows the following day, as he was one of the seven people sentenced to death for their alleged involvement in the now-famous Haymarket Riot. Rather than give the government the satisfaction of fulfilling the sentence, Lingg asked his friend to smuggle a blasting cap inside a cigar. It was his final act of defiance.

The Haymarket Riot took place on May 4, 1886, at Haymarket Square in Chicago. Labor activists organized the rally to protest the police killing of several workers during a strike the day before at the McCormick Reaper Works.[33] While the rally started off relatively peaceful, it eventually devolved into chaotic violence after someone threw a bomb at police, killing eight.

We call this era the Gilded Age, a time of unprecedented economic growth in America. But it was also a time of great tumult, as many factory workers organized to protest low wages, long hours, and dismal working conditions. Conditions created by a number of so-called robber barons who used fraud, intimidation, union busting, and extensive political connections to become titans in the railroad, oil, banking, timber, liquor, meatpacking, steel, mining, tobacco, and textile industries.[34]

This period of great change prompted many to start thinking and writing about the human toll of industry. Mark Twain and Charles Dudley Warner offered a biting critique of corporate corruption and greed in *The Gilded Age: A Tale of Today*. William Gannett, a Unitarian minister from Boston, Massachusetts, took a different position.

Gannett was a man guided by a deep and profound sense of justice. After earning a master's degree from Harvard in 1863, he went down to work with freed African Americans on the island of Port Royal in South Carolina. And when he started to see the masses suffering at work, he decided to study and write about it.

In a pamphlet called *Blessed be Drudgery*, Gannet acknowledged the difficult work and widespread suffering, but argued that rote and routine jobs could actually be the path to liberation. Specifically, he asserted that the act of committing yourself to a profession long after it's lost its appeal is one of the most powerful and transcendent human opportunities. To make the case, Gannet cited Michelangelo in saying, "Nothing makes the soul so pure, so religious, as the endeavor to create something perfect," [35] and he called drudgery "the one thing I do that gathers me together from my chaos, that concentrates me from possibilities to powers, and turns powers into achievements." To Gannet, drudgery was the gray angel of success.

The pamphlet was an instant hit. People from all professions rushed to read an encouraging and redemptive message that their suffering at work was not for naught. But what should we make of these two drastically different paths emerging from the same set of facts? The first, an anarchist willing to die to fight injustice, and the second, a minister promoting the power of perseverance through mundane work.

In *Man's Search for Meaning*, psychiatrist Viktor Frankl famously wrote that, "In some ways suffering ceases to be suffering at the moment it finds a meaning."[36] His time in a Nazi concentration camp taught him that our main motivation in life is not pleasure, as Sigmund Freud believed, nor power, as Alfred Adler believed, but meaning. Meaning is what humans need the most, especially in the hard times.

So, when we look at the stories of Louis Lingg and William Gannett through this lens, we see that they have more in common than not. Lingg's answer to the suffering of the Gilded Age was to find meaning in resistance, and for Gannett, it was meaning in persistence. In that way, both men show us that, in the wake of hard times, the end of suffering is not about which path we take, but the meaning we create.

Our suffering can cease to be suffering.

The Struggle and Spark

IT WAS 1984, AND A YOUNG ROCK musician named Bruce Springsteen was working to finish his seventh studio album at The Hit Factory in Manhattan. He had already written more than 70 songs for the record, but his manager, Jon Landau, told him he needed a hit.[37] Springsteen snapped, "I've written 70 songs. You want another one, you write it."[38]

Springsteen went back to his hotel room and picked up his guitar. At that point in life, he felt isolated from the success of *The River* four years earlier, and he was frustrated trying to write a hit single for the new record. It's why he wrote a song that night about how you can't force a creative breakthrough. A sentiment that comes through loud and clear in the chorus as Springsteen yells, "You can't start a fire without a spark."

The song "Dancing in the Dark" would go on to become the biggest hit of his life, earning him his first Grammy and helping him sell more than 30 million copies of the new album. Undoubtedly, the song is iconic. But the deep irony in the story of its creation is equally important. A man wrote a song frustrated that he couldn't force a hit, and it became his greatest.

Our struggle can be the spark that helps us dance in the dark.

A Candle or a Curse

THE HARWOOD MANUFACTURING Corporation moved its headquarters from New England to Marion, Virginia, in 1927. The company made pajamas, and this move gave them access to a number of people in the mountains of rural Virginia looking for work. They quickly hired 500 women and 100 men, and the management team felt validated. Their plan to find a quality workforce at a more reasonable price worked beautifully.

But with extremely tight margins and ever-changing technology, clothing can be a volatile industry. To keep up, the employees at Harwood frequently received new machines to master and products to make. And while the company gave bonuses and developed training courses to help people adapt to change, this process didn't go well. Many employees decided to quit rather than change the way they work, and those that did stay grew bitter toward management.

Desperate for help, in 1939, the managing director of the factory invited a psychologist named Kurt Lewin to help the company understand how to help employees navigate change. Lewin's key findings were published in a 1948 article entitled, "Overcoming Resistance to Change."[39]

It was the first of thousands of articles that would eventually be written on the topic, and not much has changed since. Workers still lose trust in their leaders and settle into a routine of doing the bare minimum to keep a paycheck.

We still vent to colleagues, let tensions flare, slow-roll change, and hope new ideas die on the vine. It's why passive resistance to change remains one of the biggest problems facing most organizations in the world today.

And it's entirely understandable. It's easy to get to a place where we spend as much time complaining about our jobs and bosses as we do actually working. And while this may not seem like a big deal, it is. It's self-inflicted spiritual violence. Just consider the now-famous progress principle put forward by Harvard researchers in 2011, which states that the most important driver of fulfillment and joy on the job is making progress in meaningful work.[40] And passive resistance is not progress.

But this point doesn't require a Harvard study. It just comes down to how we want to spend our time. In 1907, William Lonsdale Watkinson wrote that, "It is far better to light the candle than to curse the darkness."[41] When we look at our lives and the fact that we spend the majority of our time at work, it's important to remember that there is no middle ground. We can either light the candle, or curse in the dark.

The choice is ours.

The Mill Mother's Lament

IT WAS SEPTEMBER 14, 1929. Ella May Wiggins sat in the bed of a rented truck with 20 others from the National Textile Workers Union.[42] They were headed to a rally in Gaston, North Carolina, to protest the long hours, low pay, and unsafe conditions that plagued textile workers across the region. As a single (and pregnant) mom who watched four of her children die at the hands of poverty and disease, Wiggins told people that she was protesting to keep her babies alive. But their truck never made it to the rally in Gaston that day.

A group of armed men in a caravan stopped the union truck and ordered them to turn around. Though Wiggins and the others obliged, one of the armed men sped up and intentionally cut them off on their way home. The resulting collision launched most of the union members into the street, including Wiggins. Witnesses said that she was on her feet when a man named Horace Wheelus got out of his car and opened fire on the group, sending a single round through Wiggins' heart. She and her unborn child died, and the five children that she left at home would never see their mom alive again.

This would have been the end of Wiggins' story if not for her songs.

Wiggins wasn't going to that rally just to protest; she was going to sing. That year, she had written a number of different songs that emerged as the soundtrack of the labor movement in the region. Songs like "Two Little Strikers," "The Big Fat Boss and the Workers," and "All Around the Jailhouse." But there was one song in particular that really caught on. Called "Mill Mother's Lament," it was a song about the hopeless sacrifice that mill workers made to work long grueling days that still left them unable to provide for their kids.

Wiggins died before her voice could be recorded, but those songs live on today thanks to a folk musician named Margaret Larkin who took them back with her to New York City to play for sympathetic crowds in Greenwich Village.[43] The songs grew popular, and Alan Lomax, Woody Guthrie, and Pete Seeger eventually put a few of them in their book, *Hard Hitting Songs for Hard-Hit People*.

While Wiggins and those like her did eventually pave the way for better conditions and fair wages in America, there are still many left behind today. Consider the story of a 45-year-old undocumented immigrant named Martha Solorzano. To support her family, she worked in a slaughterhouse in Holcomb, Kansas, that kills 6,000 cows per day. Solorzano wasn't a permanent worker on the line; she was a contract employee working nights with the sanitation crew. Every night, she and her colleagues would arrive at 11 p.m. to wade through blood, grease, and chunks of bone to hose down the machines with scalding water and chemical disinfectants before the morning shift.

At 3:30 a.m. on July 7, 2011, Solorzano had just finished cleaning a conveyor belt on the main factory floor.

After powering the machine back on, she noticed that she forgot to wipe down a spot where fat had collected. As Solorzano reached under the moving belt to clean the area, she lost her balance, and her left hand got pulled into the machine's roller. Her forearm bones shattered, and Solorzano immediately screamed for a supervisor to shut down the line. Maintenance workers had to take the machine apart to get her free.

While Solorzano was in the hospital, a company investigator came to interview her. She told the man the accident was her fault. The company immediately fired her and denied any worker's compensation beyond the initial medical bill, even though the accident left her hand permanently disabled. Solorzano was released from the hospital and has since vanished.[44]

This is a tragic, yet timeless story. Upton Sinclair wrote a version of it in his 1906 book, *The Jungle*. The book takes place in a Chicago meatpacking plant with immigrants working under terrible conditions and a main character who gets fired after being injured on the job. The similarities are uncanny, yet not totally surprising given that America still averages two amputations per week from slaughterhouse accidents.[45] History does indeed repeat itself when it comes to those hard-hit people in hard-hitting jobs.

We are pretty good at celebrating the heroes who rush into a fire, jump on a grenade, or pull someone off the tracks. But we often overlook the droves of unsung mothers and fathers who suffer silently at work for their children. People like Martha Solorzano who risk everything to earn $202 per week so that their kids have a chance to grow up in America. They are heroes, every last one of them.

Ella May Wiggins was buried in an unmarked grave in Gaston County, North Carolina. On the 50th anniversary of her death, the local AFL-CIO installed a large marble cross on her grave that read, "She died carrying the torch of social justice." A torch that still burns today thanks to Martha Solorzano and selfless workers across the world.

Heroes, every last one of them.

Dreams in the Dark Mansion

ON JUNE 23, 1993, DR. ANDREW WILES walked to the front of a lecture hall in Cambridge, England. He was there to give the last in a series of talks that he titled "Modular Forms, Elliptic Curves, and Galois Representations." This was standard practice for Wiles, a professor of mathematics at Princeton University who studied number theory.

But about 20 minutes into the talk, the presentation took a turn. After presenting a seemingly routine set of mathematical conclusions, Wiles looked up and said, "Implies Fermat's Last Theorem." This was a really big deal. Fermat's Last Theorem was the world's most famous mathematical hypothesis, and it remained unsolved for more than 350 years. It was the white whale of mathematics, and many before Wiles squandered their prime years in pursuit of the proof.

French mathematician Pierre de Fermat first wrote his theorem in the margins of his copy of an old Greek text called *Arithmetica* in 1637. The theorem states that no equation of the form $x^n + y^n = z^n$ has a whole-number solution when n is greater than two. But rather than show a proof for the theorem, Fermat simply wrote, "I have discovered a truly marvelous demonstration of this proposition that this margin is too narrow to contain."[46] That is, I know the answer, but I don't have enough space to write it. So began modern math's hardest problem.

Wiles first encountered the theorem in a math book that he found at the library when he was 10 years old, and he had long fantasized about solving it. He considered attempting the proof for his doctoral thesis at Cambridge University, but his advisor convinced him to avoid the tempting dead-end path. Instead, Wiles studied elliptic curves, earned his doctorate, and eventually joined the faculty at Princeton in 1981.[47]

Life at Princeton treated Wiles well. He married, published meaningful papers, and enjoyed teaching classes. But in 1986, Wiles was sipping iced tea when his friend casually mentioned that a number theorist from the University of California in Berkeley had laid out a new path for proving Fermat's Last Theorem. This mathematician, Ken Ribet, discovered that in order to prove Fermat's theorem, one need only prove a new conjecture from two young researchers in Tokyo called the Taniyama-Shimura Conjecture.

And while the Taniyama-Shimura Conjecture wasn't necessarily any easier to prove, Wiles was electrified. He later told the public television program NOVA, "I knew that moment the course of my life was changing."[48] Wiles abandoned all of his other research, cut himself off from the rest of the world, and spent the next seven years working alone in his attic. He was going to prove Fermat's Last Theorem, and this time he wasn't going to let anyone talk him out of it.

From that day on, Wiles discussed his work with only one person: his wife. For the first two years, he did nothing but immerse himself in the problem, trying to figure out how to begin. Then he worked in fits and starts, slowly chipping away at what would become his proof. Wiles later explained the journey as follows:

> *"Perhaps I could best describe my experience of doing mathematics in terms of entering a dark mansion. One goes into the first room, and it's dark, completely dark. One stumbles around bumping into the furniture, and gradually, you learn where each piece of furniture is, and finally, after six months or so, you find the light switch. You turn it on, and suddenly, it's all illuminated. You can see exactly where you were. At the*

beginning of September, I was sitting here at this desk, when suddenly, totally unexpectedly, I had this incredible revelation."[49]

And that was it. When the lights came on, Wiles had solved Fermat's Last Theorem. So, he took the stage at that conference in Cambridge in June 1993 to tell the world. And despite the understated reveal, news spread fast. The *New York Times* put the story on the front page, *People Magazine* named him one of "The 25 Most Intriguing People of the Year," and Gap asked him to model a new line of jeans. (He declined.)[50] It was validation for taking the leap that most wouldn't. A leap that could have taken his best years and left him with nothing to show for it.[51]

Stories like Wiles' are fuel. Human beings encounter impossible dreams that they cannot shake, and when everything and everyone tells them to move on to a more sensible path, they persist against all odds. They put their heads down and struggle, sometimes for years, to reach their goal. They are Amelia Earhart across the Atlantic, Edmund Hillary atop Everest, or Roger Bannister breaking the four-minute mile.

But on the journey to life's biggest accomplishments, there will be dark days when it feels like everything's falling apart. In those moments, our only hope to make it through is our strength of will, not technical skill. So keep this story close—you'll need it in the dark mansion before those lights come on.

III. HUMAN THINGS

"There's definitely, definitely, definitely no logic to human behavior."
—Björk

When the Mask Becomes Your Face

YUSUF ABDI ALI WAS DRIVING TWO passengers for Uber in his white Nissan Altima on a sunny afternoon in May 2019. By all accounts, Ali was good at his job. Customers awarded him a cumulative rating of 4.89 out of 5 stars, which helped him reach the elite Uber Pro Diamond status. Given where Ali came from, this could have been an inspirational tale of man overcoming adversity.

Ali was from Somalia, a country that has been embroiled in different iterations of a civil war since the mid-1980s. Collectively, these conflicts have killed more than 500,000 people and made Somalia one of the most dangerous places on earth. Ali was lucky to get out; after a brief asylum in Canada, he was eventually granted status as a permanent resident in the United States in 1996. He has lived in Northern Virginia ever since.

Which brings us to that day in May 2019. Ali didn't know it then, but the two passengers getting into his vehicle were CNN reporters. They were there to see if it was true. Was an alleged war criminal from Somalia actually living and working in Northern Virginia as an Uber driver? They got in the car, asked the driver his name, and verified that he was indeed the notorious Yusuf Abdi Ali, also known as Colonel Tukeh.[52]

Turns out Ali, the Uber Pro Diamond driver, is also allegedly one of the most ruthless commanders of the

20-year Siad Barre dictatorship, personally responsible for the detention, cruel treatment, and death of thousands of people.[53] This includes soaking civilians in oil and lighting them on fire and dragging others by a rope behind his car. Ali was not a good man.

This story will leave most of us longing for at least some semblance of justice. As it stands, there may not be much. While Ali did lose his job, he is not currently facing any criminal charges, and there was only one civil lawsuit in Virginia filed by a former torture victim. Jurisdiction issues can make the arc of justice especially long in cases like these. But beyond the legalities, this story does beg one big question: How did one of the most violent war criminals in recent history become such a polite and highly rated Uber driver?

Yusuf Abdi Ali was not the first to walk the path from war criminal to peaceful employee. The brutal Nazi Franz Stangl went from overseeing the murder of one million at death camps in Poland to working at a Volkswagen factory in São Paulo. The Liberian General Joshua Milton Blahyi and his battalion of child soldiers killed more than 20,000 before he became a Christian minister.[54]

While we don't want to understate their responsibility for these terrible crimes, social psychologist Erving Goffman does offer a compelling rationale for radical transformations like these. In his 1959 book, *The Presentation of Self in Everyday Life*, Goffman argued that social encounters are really just theatrical performances.[55] And that most of us shape those performances to reflect the norms, values, and traditions of our audience.

In other words, we reflect the company we keep. Apply this concept to your workplace. If you work somewhere filled with gossip, infighting, or inefficient meetings, your social psychological instincts will likely pressure you to do the same. And if your workplace is supportive, collaborative, and high-achieving, you probably will be too. Workplace culture doesn't just shape organizations, it shapes us.

And while it's not war crimes for most, workplace social pressure can atrophy skills, dampen spirits, and put dreams to bed. That's the power of group dynamics. The trick is to recognize these changes in yourself when they happen, which is incredibly hard to do.

That is why Goffman offered this ominous warning: "Choose your self-presentations carefully, for what starts out as a mask may become your face."

May we never let our work make us something we are not.

The Conflicts That Kill

IN 2000, Nokia's research lab built a full-color touchscreen phone with a single button beneath the screen.[56] This was seven years before Apple's first smartphone, and many have said that the Nokia prototype was as good as the first-generation iPhone. This was not totally unexpected, given Nokia's tradition of changing with the times.

Founded in 1865 by a Finnish engineer named Fredrik Idestam, Nokia first sold paper, then electricity, and then rubber galoshes. As the market continued to evolve, the company excelled at finding success with new products. So much so that by the 1990s, Nokia was the largest communications company in the world.

But we already know this story, don't we? We know that Nokia failed to ship a viable smartphone, and that the iPhone eventually killed its business, with more than 40,000 people losing their jobs. But why? Why, if they had a solid smartphone a full seven years before Apple released theirs?

Because Nokia's fall wasn't about technology, it was about people. Infighting between different departments prevented decision-makers from ever seeing the prototype. That is, the one product that could have saved more than 40,000 jobs never even got a look from senior executives because people couldn't get along. That's how human conflict kills companies.

We've all seen it. The tension, the meeting after the meeting, the endless emails, the hours venting to friends and family, and even the occasional blowout. At the end of the day, this unnecessary human suffering and wasted time costs organizations hundreds of billions of dollars each year.

But what can we do? No list in any book can guarantee success, but here's a place to start:

- **Air it out.** There is a reason that most boxing matches end with a hug and traditional wars end with a treaty. Active conflict fuels peace. At work, however, conflict is typically passive, and passive battles never end. Why? Because if nobody acknowledges that there is a conflict, you can't stop it. The first step is for all parties to directly air their grievances with all those involved. From here, you can uncover the root cause of the conflict and have some hope that it might end.

- **Break the cycle with an olive branch.** Most conflict is cyclical. There are a series of call-and-response behaviors on each side that trigger a reaction from the other. In his book, *The Evolution of Cooperation*, Robert Axelrod found that an unexpected olive branch can actually break the cycle of conflict.[57] And those who consistently extend olive branches, even if unreciprocated, are more likely to find success with long-term relationships and negotiations.

- **Cooperate on a new venture together.** The most effective peacebuilding initiatives in the

Israeli-Palestinian conflict have been joint infrastructure and water projects. While the practice is no panacea, getting away from the mediating table to work together on a new initiative can be a great way to redefine the dynamic and build new cooperative bridges.

- **Connect as humans, not coworkers**: In 2016, Google conducted a study to uncover the secret ingredient in its most successful teams. After nearly two years, the company discovered that the key to a high-performing team is a concept called psychological safety, which is a shared confidence that the team will not embarrass, reject, or punish you for speaking up.[58] How do you get there? Whether it's the pain of a divorce, the joy of climbing a mountain, or the magic of falling in love, the first step to psychological safety is to share personal stories to find shared humanity.

So, that's it. Most of us won't have a meteoric rise like Nokia, but we can try to avoid the misstep that made it fall. We can build more bridges than we burn.

Lessons From a Miner Celebrity

A MAN NAMED ALEXEI STAKHANOV and his three colleagues entered a Soviet coal mine in Donbass at 10 p.m. on August 30, 1935.[59] Dressed in thick canvas suits, boots, and helmets, they were accompanied by a journalist and the local communist party boss. This was no normal shift—these men were going to make history.

The mine in Donbass was one of the worst-performing in the region, and Stakhanov had an idea about how to turn it around. During these years, miners used picks to break the coal loose, then loaded it on carts so that it could be pulled out of the shaft by horses called pit ponies. Stakhanov suggested having one miner constantly picking coal while another loaded the cart, a third supported the roof from collapse with timbers, and a fourth led the pony in and out. He also decided to use a new 33-pound pneumatic mining drill instead of a pick.[60]

With this new method, the crew set a world production record for coal, drilling 102 tons in just six hours—14 times more than what was typically mined during a shift. In a region still recovering from a devastating famine that killed millions, good news was hard to come by. People devoured the stories written about Stakhanov and the team, and he became a national hero overnight.

This story inspired workers from different trades, and nearly every industry soon saw similar feats of production. Aleksandr Busygin forged 1,115 crankshafts in a single shift in the Gorky automotive plant, a locomotive engineer named Pyotr Krivonos increased the average speed of freight trains to that of passenger trains, and Pasha Angelina formed an all-female brigade of tractor operators that exceeded all previous production numbers.[61]

They called themselves the Stakhanovites, and they took pride in working above and beyond. The movement eventually gained the attention of Joseph Stalin, who hosted and spoke at the First All-Union Conference of Stakhanovites in Moscow in November 1935. There, he declared the Stakhanovites movement to be evidence that socialism would defeat capitalism, as it could inspire a higher level of pride and productivity than money alone.[62] *Time* magazine even featured Alexei Stakhanov on the cover of a December 1935 issue to introduce the movement and its achievements.

We may have never heard of Alexei Stakhanov, but in an age obsessed with productivity, this story is still familiar to us. Whether it's Timothy Ferriss and *The 4-Hour Workweek*, Alan Lakein and *How to Get Control of Your Time and Your Life*, Steven R. Covey and *The 7 Habits of Highly Effective People*, or Charles Duhigg and *Smarter, Faster, Better*, there are no shortage of books spreading the religion of productivity. They are bestsellers because so many of us want to do and be more.

The problem is that doing more *doesn't* make us more. Consider the productivity guru Merlin Mann. In summer 2007, he presented a new personal productivity idea called

"Inbox Zero" to a small group at Google. It was a radically simple concept: Every time you visit your email inbox, you should systematically process it to zero (e.g., send a reply, add an item to your to-do list, or delete the message).

The idea caught on like wildfire. Hundreds of thousands watched the video of his talk, people started relentlessly managing their inboxes, and Mann traveled the world delivering keynote speeches and consulting services to large organizations. Naturally, a publisher offered him a book deal.

But the book never came out. Mann found that his boundless devotion to writing about productivity caused him to lose sight of the biggest priorities in his life. Namely, spending time with his three-year-old daughter. Mann also discovered that, despite any initial productivity gains, Inbox Zero was actually increasing stress and anxiety for early adopters. In the face of all of this, he cancelled the book project and forever walked away from what he now calls "the productivity racket."[63]

Friedrich Nietzsche once famously said that, "Haste is universal because everyone is in flight from himself." Even in his time, Nietzsche saw the pitfalls of pursuing excessive productivity. And George Orwell did too. He used Stakhanov as the basis for the workhorse Boxer in his 1945 book *Animal Farm*.[64] A loyal and strong horse, Boxer believed that any problem on the farm could be solved if he just worked harder. So he never quit, and that's why he eventually got injured and died.

Stakhanov suffered a similar fate. After Stalin died, the new Soviet leader, Nikita Khrushchev, saw no need to keep Stakhanov in Moscow with the Coal Ministry. He ordered Stakhanov back to Donbass alone, essentially in exile.[65] Without his work, he slipped into a deep depression, drank continuously, and eventually died alone of a stroke.

The year after Stakhanov passed, the citizens of the town where he started his career changed the city's name from Kadievka to Stakhanov. He is the only blue-collar worker in history to have a city named on his behalf. May it always honor the heart behind his hard work, and remind us that we are more than what we do.

Revolution in the Air

TOUSSAINT L'OUVERTURE WAS BORN into slavery in Saint-Domingue roughly around 1743. At the time, the Caribbean island exported more sugar and coffee and imported more captive Africans than anywhere in the world. From 1783 through 1791, more than 790,000 enslaved Africans worked the plantations in the French colony,[66] accounting for one-third of the entire Atlantic slave trade.[67]

Life was hell in Saint-Domingue, and roughly half of those enslaved on the island died from yellow fever within a year of arriving. Those who did survive faced brutal treatment from plantation owners—including cutting off ears, pouring boiling sugar over bodies, and lighting mouths filled with gunpowder on fire. L'Ouverture's destiny was statistically bleak.

That being said, he did encounter more opportunity than most on the island. At an early age, L'Ouverture was put in charge of the livestock at the Breda Plantation, which he leveraged to gain experience as a horse-trainer and veterinarian.[68] He learned to read and gained access to the plantation's library, where he immersed himself in the writings of Greek philosophers, Julius Caesar, and Guillaume Raynal, a French Enlightenment thinker who opposed slavery.[69]

And, in 1776, the owner of the Breda Plantation granted L'Ouverture freedom at the age of 33. He stayed on as a paid employee, got married, had children, and began to acquire property and wealth. While L'Ouverture did find some peace in his new circumstances, he refused to ignore the human suffering that surrounded him—and he wasn't alone. A revolution was in the air.

In August 1791, a group of Africans gathered in the forest at Bois Caïman to perform a vodou ritual that would launch the largest enslaved peoples rebellion in history. Over the next few months, they embarked on a series of chaotic attacks that left the plains and plantations of northern Saint-Domingue on fire. By the end of the year, L'Ouverture emerged as the leader of the rebel army and, over the next decade, his forces would face the armies of France, Britain, Spain, and then France again. More than

350,000 people would die, most of them rebels.

Napoleon captured L'Ouverture in 1802 and brought him to an exceptionally harsh prison in France. He died a few months later on April 7, 1803. L'Ouverture didn't know it then, but his army was only nine months from defeating Napoleon. On January 1, 1804, the last of Napoleon's troops retreated, and the rebels claimed victory. They named their country Haiti, and theirs remains the most successful enslaved people's rebellion in history.

Many see this as a story about the power of perseverance, gains to be made with guerilla tactics, and the difficulty of defeating a truly inspired movement. After all, L'Ouverture was able to lead a group of untrained and ill-equipped soldiers to defeat three of the world's most powerful armies. But there is a key takeaway missing from that list. For that, we have to go back to his time in the library at the Breda Plantation.

There, L'Ouverture read about how Julius Caesar often incorporated conquered enemies into the Roman Empire as citizens, not prisoners. How Caesar did not force former combatants to shed all aspects of their old culture, but asked them to bring the best of what they were to Roman society. This strategy became a source of the Roman Empire's strength and rapid innovation, and L'Ouverture never forgot it.

That's why he incorporated many captured French and British soldiers into his own ranks as leaders and generals. Like Caesar, this was not a move to placate the enemy; it was an opportunity to grow stronger. Which brings us to L'Ouverture's biggest lesson: Don't let your anger live longer than the war.

Human conflict is inevitable. We are too fickle, temperamental, and fragile to avoid it. The gossip, groupthink, raised voices, and occasional fistfight bear forth a tit-for-tat cycle of conflict in our interactions that can be eerily similar to war. In the heat of those moments, L'Ouverture reminds us that anyone can fire a shot to make a war begin, but only the great know how to extend the hand when they win.

And with that Toussaint L'Ouverture didn't just liberate Haiti, he liberated us all.

The Promises We Keep

DTE ENERGY HAD A CULTURE PROBLEM. In 2005, the Michigan power company suffered from low employee engagement and declining metrics in everything from productivity to customer satisfaction. Gerry Anderson was there to do something about it. As the newly hired CEO, he launched a massive change initiative with training for employees, new incentives, and increased management oversight.

The leading-edge corporate change initiative didn't work. While the higher expectations and increased oversight did improve productivity, employee morale remained low over the next few years. And right as Anderson and his team were trying to figure out a new approach, the global economy collapsed. DTE Energy lost nearly $200 million in revenue overnight.[70] Culture change would have to wait; this ship was sinking.

The company's 2008 financial strategy went up in flames, and Anderson's senior leaders told him the only way to stay afloat was to lay off thousands of people. With genuine affinity for the employees of DTE, Anderson couldn't bear the thought. Instead, he recorded a message for DTE's 10,000 employees. He told them the company had lost $200 million, it was getting worse, and the only option he and his team could come up with was to lay off thousands. A wave of sadness and fear swept over the people watching that video.

But then the Hail Mary came. Anderson looked directly into the camera and said, "I'll make this commitment to you: The last thing we'll do is lay anybody off. But, in return, I need you to bring your energy, your focus, and your intensity to our work like you never have before. And if you do that, if all 10,000 of us do that together, we can fix this."[71] Anderson didn't have a plan, just a promise: Good or bad, we're in this together.

When he refused to move forward with the layoffs, Anderson put his job on the line too. No one would have blamed him for letting people go in the wake of the greatest recession since 1929, but many, most notably the board and shareholders, would now blame him if this experiment didn't work. Anderson bet his job to save theirs, and that's what made his promise real.

Real enough to fuel change. The people of DTE became more innovative and creative than ever before. One team replacing a power plant control system realized that they could repurpose every part except for the circuit board. They completed the $30 million repair for just $3 million. Creative solutions like this sparked across the organization, and the company, surrounded by shuttering steel mills and auto plants, started to turn things around.

The shift happened so fast that Anderson thought their financial models were broken. The company tripled their stock price in a few years, prompting the governor to ask DTE to invest more money in Michigan suppliers. The company redirected over $922 million into the state's economy. Meaning the people of DTE didn't only save their jobs, they saved thousands of those around them. A promise kept, indeed.

Anderson tried for years before the recession to change the culture of DTE. He had the change initiative, incentives, and communications strategy designed by experts in organizational transformation. It just didn't work. And that's because they forgot the most important thing: Driving real change requires that leaders have as much on the line as their people. Good or bad, we're in this together.

It's a point made most vividly by General James Mattis. In April 2004, he climbed into an armored vehicle to meet with Iraqi leaders. On the way, insurgents ambushed the convoy and a firefight ensued. Despite the fact that he was a general in command of several thousand soldiers, Mattis drew his weapon, got in the dirt, and exchanged fire.[72] When the battle was done, the convoy drove on to its destination, and General Mattis walked into that negotiating room wearing a uniform soaked in blood. Good or bad, we're in this together.

To the promises we keep.

A New Rite of Spring

ON MARCH 2, 1959, SIX YOUNG MEN walked into a converted Greek Orthodox Church at 207 East 30th Street in New York City. They arrived, expectations high, to record an album with a man named Miles Davis. The lineup featured Julian "Cannonball" Adderley on alto saxophone, Bill Evans and Wynton Kelly on piano, Paul Chambers on bass, Jimmy Cobb on drums, and John Coltrane on tenor sax.

Typically in those days, session musicians were given sheet music or tablature to review, they would practice a song until they got it down, and only then would they record the track and move on to the next. But Davis didn't have any sheet music or complete songs that day. Instead, he gave the group a rough sketch of the first three songs on a single sheet of manuscript paper.

Davis wanted the group to improvise and play in an experimental style called modal jazz. This approach shifts the structure of a song away from chord progressions to a limited number of modes, which are particular musical scales. This may not mean much to most of us, but it was a revolutionary move. Modal jazz gives the soloist much more freedom to create new melodies, rhythms, and emotions. It opened up infinite possibilities.

In only nine hours, the group recorded five songs that clocked just under 46 minutes. They knew the album was good, but no one expected what came next. Columbia Records released *Kind of Blue* on August 17, 1959, and word quickly spread: Miles Davis and his group had just single-handedly reinvented jazz music.

The album sold more than five million copies and remains in print today. Quincy Jones called it his "daily orange juice," Donald Fagen from Steely Dan described it as "the Bible" of music, and Pink Floyd pianist Richard Wright said the album influenced the whole structure of *The Dark Side of the Moon*.[73] It's a record that shaped the future of music.

But why this album? The first thing to note is that it was not the album that Davis intended to create. He envisioned making a record that felt like the experience he had when he was 6 years old walking home from church with his cousin in Arkansas.[74] A walk where he heard bits and pieces of gospel music from the houses that they passed along the way. But that's not at all where it landed—because he didn't actually write the songs; everyone in that room did.

Kind of Blue isn't remarkable because Miles Davis was a genius. It's remarkable because he knew how to build an environment that would create genius. In his 1989 autobiography, Davis wrote, "If you put a musician in a place where he has to do something different from what he does all the time ... that's where great art and music happens."[75] And how do you create a place in jazz where the musicians have to do something new? You work with people who think and play much differently than you.

Enter John Coltrane.

While Davis and Coltrane may seem similar on the surface, their approach to music couldn't be more different. Davis was the son of a dentist, graced with the opportunity to pursue music from a young age, which helped him land a spot with Charlie Parker's famous quintet at the age of 19. Coltrane, on the other hand, lost every male in his family by the age of 13, which caused great financial and emotional hardship. He turned to music for solace, and his career progressed slowly.

Coltrane studied music exercise books and practiced everywhere he could, whether on the bus, in his hotel, or backstage. Davis didn't like the formality of all that. Instead, he would write out chord sequences on matchbooks, ruminating for hours on one musical puzzle. Coltrane was quiet and reserved, while Davis was ever the extrovert. But on stage the two would switch roles, Coltrane playing loud and long solos while Davis aimed for more subtle and short runs. It was this tension between Davis and the Trane that inspired the transformative tunes on *Kind of Blue*.

Davis understood intuitively what recent research in social science and psychology tells us: Diversity is powerful. Not because it drives cohesion, but because it drives conflict—a conflict of ideas.[76] That is, by nature we are more skeptical of ideas that come from people who aren't like us, and that skepticism causes diverse groups to ask the hard questions that need to be answered to defeat groupthink and do world-class work.

That same body of research found that diverse groups may feel less comfortable at first. When we are with people who don't share our background, traditions, experiences, language, or education, it can take longer to bond and define a cohesive group dynamic. But as we look at this example of Davis and Coltrane, we see that working on a diverse team may be less comfortable, but exactly what we need to create great things.

One year after they recorded *Kind of Blue*, Davis asked the band to join him on a European tour. Coltrane wanted to quit the band to branch out on his own, and he had already booked some solo shows. But Davis managed to convince him to stay through the end of the European run. Coltrane wasn't happy about it, and everyone knew it. He sat quietly brooding for the entire ride to the first show in Paris.

But when they took the stage at the Olympia Theatre,

Coltrane exploded. A burst of notes on top of notes with a frantic and dissonant energy that captured the crowd. It was loud and chaotic with mid-range cries, high-pitched shrieks, and other sounds that no saxophone had made before. Referring back to the 1913 debut of Igor Stravinsky's riot-causing ballet, reporter Charles Estienne wrote the following day in *France-Observateur*: "… this first day of spring, March 21, was the opening night of the 'Rite of Spring' of modern jazz."[77]

Music producer Steve Berkowitz, who co-produced the bootleg box set from the final Davis-Coltrane tour, may have expressed the power of their partnership best: "In this binary era, when people seem to be for or against things, we all could use this display of different minds working together to create something beautiful."[78]

To Miles Davis and John Coltrane, for teaching us that genius is not born from the things we share, but the things that set us apart.

IV. MEANING

"I'm sure I could write endlessly about nothing. If only I had nothing to say."

—Patti Smith

The Smell of Cedar in the Air

JOE RANTZ WAS 10 YEARS OLD WHEN his family kicked him out the first time. It was 1924. His father had remarried after Rantz's mother died seven years earlier and, for no obvious reason, his stepmother Thula couldn't stand him. So Rantz started sleeping in the local schoolhouse in Sequim, Washington, fishing, hunting, and working odd jobs to feed himself.

Though his father eventually did insist that Joe be allowed to return home, his reprieve didn't last long. At 15, he came home from school to find his dad, stepmom, and four younger siblings driving away. Joe was alone, and this time for two years. He moved into a half-finished cabin in the woods, surviving by logging timber, clearing tree stumps, baling hay, and building fences.

Finally, Rantz caught a break. His oldest brother and his wife invited him to live with them in Seattle for his senior year. Rantz enrolled in Roosevelt High School, and with newfound extra time, he thrived in his studies and took up sports. One day in gymnastics practice, he was doing a routine on the high bar when a man named Al Ulbrickson walked in. Ulbrickson, the University of Washington rowing coach, saw Rantz's muscular build and encouraged him to enroll in the university and try out for his crew team.

There were no scholarships for college sports in those days, so Rantz knew that if he wanted to go to the University of Washington, he would have to pay his own way. After graduating, he worked for 15 months on two Works Project Administration jobs—first manually digging and paving highways, then rappelling down cliffs to clear rock for the Grand Coulee Dam. He averaged 60 hours a week.

So began the rise of the Boys of '36. Rantz made the freshmen rowing team when he enrolled in the University of Washington in 1934. And by studying hard and rowing harder, he would go on to make the varsity boat in his sophomore year. The rest of Rantz's tale is legendary. He and the underrated University of Washington crew team—a ragtag collection of sons of dockworkers, loggers, farmers, and manual laborers—beat every single elite college team, including their rivals at the University of California at Berkeley, Harvard, Yale, Oxford, and Cambridge. The team then bested those same squads to earn a spot on the U.S. Olympic Team in the 1936 Summer Games in Berlin.

There, in front of 75,000 fans and in spite of illness, a delayed start, and crowds so loud they couldn't hear the coxswain's calls, the Boys of '36 made history. Rowing at 44 strokes-per-minute—the fastest ever—the American team overcame a last-place start to sail past Adolf Hitler and his top lieutenants and claim the gold by six-tenths of a second. Six-tenths of a second.

There is a common thread throughout Rantz's journey from tragedy to triumph. Whether he was living alone in the woods at 10 years old, working 60 hours a week digging ditches, or winning gold with one of the best rowing teams in history, Rantz was somehow able to find as much peace and fulfillment in the lows of life as the highs. It's a skill that was common in his generation, but maybe not so much in ours.

Consider our feelings about work. Employee engagement today remains staggeringly low. Since Gallup started tracking the number in 2000, employee disengagement in America has hovered around 70 percent.[79] This means that, despite the fact that so many of us have more economic and employment opportunities than Rantz's generation, the vast majority of American workers have found little fulfillment and joy in their work in the last 20 years. This raises an obvious question. Why is more opportunity leaving so many less fulfilled?

Fyodor Dostoevsky offers one response in his 1864 short novella *Notes From Underground*, a fictional memoir of a retired mid-level Russian bureaucrat struggling to find meaning in his life. Dostoevsky wrote the book as a warning for what he saw as the greatest threat to Russia: a growing obsession in America and Western Europe with the idea that every person should live to maximize their happiness and self-fulfillment.

While the concept sounds wonderful on its surface, Dostoevsky feared one big downside. Sometimes the least fulfilled lives are those spent searching for fulfillment. That's because you have to *do* something to be fulfilled, not just think about it. Dostoevsky's main character spent more time thinking about his life and its meaning than actually living it. So, each day devolved into a barrage of unmet expectations and an ocean of paralyzing thoughts.

Like Dostoevsky's bureaucrat, we face a tantalizing burden disguised as opportunity: the freedom to ask life's biggest questions (e.g., Is this my passion? Am I fulfilled? Does my job matter?). But no amount of thinking will bring a satisfying answer to these questions, nor will any employee recognition program, professional development opportunity, or manager give you the meaning you seek in your work. True engagement comes from within—from disciplined action, not never-ending analysis. And that's why employee disengagement is not a crisis of management; it's a crisis of the mind.

When Joe Rantz was living in that cabin in the woods, he and a friend would find scrap cedar limbs that lumber companies left behind. They would strip the bark and split the wood to make cedar shakes. It was difficult and repetitive work, but Rantz soon fell in love with it. He talked about that work on his deathbed with the author Daniel James Brown.

Rantz described how much he loved it when the wood finally split. The spicy-sweet smell of cedar in the air and the unpredictable, yet always beautiful, patterns of orange, burgundy, and cream in the grain. He said that shaping cedar satisfied him down to his core and gave him peace. Pretty good perspective for a kid whose family left him alone in the woods.

The engagement we seek is within.

When We Don't Know What We're Doing

ON FEBRUARY 15, 2006, 40 SOLDIERS wearing what appeared to be U.S. Army uniforms climbed a hill overlooking some bamboo huts in the South Pacific. One of them raised an American flag up a tree, and they began marching down the hill. But as they got closer, an odd picture emerged. The rifles were really bamboo rods, their uniforms homemade, their feet bare, and their chests painted with the red letters, "USA."[80]

Welcome to John Frum Day on the remote Tanna Island.

The island's John Frum movement is an example of what anthropologists call a "cargo cult." Many of these groups formed in villages across the South Pacific after hundreds of thousands of American troops poured onto the islands during World War II. While there, the Americans exposed indigenous populations to modern technology, vast material wealth, and a seemingly endless supply of jeeps, radios, motorcycles, canned meat, and candy. But when the Americans left, the supply runs stopped.

That's when things got interesting. Many of the indigenous people had grown to like the modern amenities that came with the American way. So they organized into small groups to try to get the supply runs started again. Having never seen airplanes or advanced technology before the Americans arrived, the people of Tanna Island attributed the shipments to magical forces. Magic that would have to be summoned by the rigid set of rituals they witnessed every day.

So these groups cleared dirt runways, built bamboo traffic control towers, carved headsets from wood, made Army uniforms, built bamboo planes, lit the runways with fire at night, and mimicked the daily movements of the American soldiers (including sitting at desks to talk on wooden radios, shuffling papers between buildings, and staffing runways 24 hours a day). They worked and prayed, but no shipments came.

No doubt these are fascinating, and heartbreaking, tales. Many of us would like the chance to tell those people their work is futile. That their bamboo planes will never fly, that the goods they seek are made in far-off factories for a price, that radios need electricity to reach the outside world. Because with that clarity, maybe those people could devote their time to more important things—like building their communities in their own way.

But before we dwell on the tragic consequences of their confusion, we should take a moment to consider ours. What if we need clarity as much as them? What if our workplace rituals are becoming just as confused and detached from reality as theirs? The idea is not as far-fetched as it seems.

We face more complexity and confusion at work today than ever before. In the time since World War II, the number of processes, committees, decision-making forums, and procedures at large organizations has increased by a factor of 35.[81] The average office worker now spends at least six hours a day on email and wastes roughly half of the time spent in meetings.

So, it's no surprise that an IBM study found that more than 1,500 CEOs said the largest challenge that they face is complexity.[82] Or that 74 percent of respondents to a 2014 Deloitte survey rated their workplace as either "complex" or "highly complex."[83] And when most CEOs and employees agree that their workplace is overly complex, nearly every metric for success suffers, including employee engagement, efficiency, profit, and productivity.

And that's how we landed in a place where we often write reports that no one reads, have meetings that meander to nowhere, build slide decks that never get used, write email chains that don't end, and use jargon that no one really understands.

Who's building the bamboo planes now?

Just like those soldiers marching with their homemade bayonets, we risk trading the best of what we could be for work filled with confusion and complexity. So if we do nothing else, let it be this: May we only use the words we know, do the work we believe in, and always remember what we're capable of.

To the people of Tanna Island, and what they saw in us.

Why You Will Only Tell Six Good Stories in Your Life

IN MAY 1945, A 22-YEAR-OLD SOLDIER wrote a letter home to his parents in Indianapolis, Indiana. He described being captured by a German panzer division in what is now called the Battle of the Bulge. The soldier and his unit were loaded onto unheated box cars for a 10-day train ride to a prisoner-of-war camp south of Dresden. After five months watching fellow prisoners die from starvation, abuse, and Allied air raids, the soldier and eight others stole a German truck and drove for eight days until they reached Soviet territory. It was time to go home.

When the soldier got there, he married his high school sweetheart, Jane Marie, and they moved west to enroll in the University of Chicago. Likely influenced by the human extremes that he witnessed during the war, he signed up for a joint undergraduate/graduate program in anthropology. After a few years in the program, he wrote a master's thesis that he called, "The Fluctuations Between Good and Evil in Simple Tales." The premise: All stories have shapes, and the great ones look alike.

The idea is that if you create a graph where the horizontal axis represents time and the vertical axis represents the fortune of the main character, you can map every story ever told. And when that student started doing this, he saw that the greatest stories had similar shapes. For example, Cinderella and the New Testament are roughly identical.

The student finished his thesis and excitedly presented it to the faculty at the university—who rejected it on the basis that it was not anthropology at all. With no money and a small child to support, he decided to walk away without a degree. He called his brother who worked at General Electric, got a job writing in the public relations department, and started writing stories of his own on the side.

His name was Kurt Vonnegut.

Vonnegut's rejected thesis helped him go on to become one of the most famous authors in American history. Because whether it was *Cat's Cradle*, *Slaughterhouse-Five*, *Player Piano*, or any of the other books that Vonnegut wrote, he carefully mapped the shape of every story he ever told.

This is also Hollywood's greatest secret. It's no coincidence that the first four *Rocky* movies all have the same shape: 1) Rocky finds some initial success; 2) tragedy strikes and he faces a seemingly impossible task; 3) Rocky works and trains harder than any human ever could; and 4) Rocky wins the fight. It's the Cinderella story: rise then fall then rise again.

Sixty-nine years after Vonnegut put forth his theory to an unimpressed faculty committee, researchers from the University of Vermont and the University of Adelaide validated his thesis in a study on the shapes of stories. The team used artificial intelligence to digitally map more than 2,000 works of fiction.[84] Their first finding was that the great stories have similar shapes. (Hat tip, Vonnegut.) Their second

finding was that there are just six main story arcs:
- Rags to Riches (rise)
- Riches to Rags (fall)
- Man in a Hole (fall then rise)
- Icarus (rise then fall)
- Cinderella (rise then fall then rise)
- Oedipus (fall then rise then fall)

This means that every one of us holds the same key to powerful storytelling as Vonnegut and Hollywood screenwriters. Whether it's a pitch for a new idea, a presentation to the colleagues, or the launch of a new strategy, you can bring your message to life by deliberately shaping the story you tell. And understanding these six main story arcs is the only place to start.

Back in 1945, Kurt Vonnegut ended his letter to his parents with this prophetic statement: "I've too damned much to say, the rest will have to wait."[85] Luckily for us, he found out just how to say it. Now we can too.

Your story awaits.

The Song of '68

OTIS REDDING WAS HIDING OUT on a houseboat in Sausalito, California, in August 1967. He was in town for a string of shows at a jazz club called Basin Street West in

San Francisco, and the promoter let him stay on the boat to escape the throngs of fans that he would have encountered at a hotel in the city. Redding spent six quiet days there, mostly sitting on the dock with an acoustic guitar, watching ferries cross the bay. He wrote the words for a chorus and verse, and most of a song on the guitar.

It was nothing like his previous work. This song was heavy, and it's probably because Redding was going through a lot at the time. After finding initial success with a string of traditional soul ballads, he wanted to do something different. Redding had spent the summer listening to *Sgt. Pepper's Lonely Hearts Club Band* on repeat, and it inspired him to focus more on the lyrics of his songs.[86] So, he sat on that dock and wrote a sad song about an overwhelmed man far from home, hopeless in the face of loneliness.

When Redding finally entered the studio in November 1967, he sounded as good as he ever had. And as Redding recorded the song with his band, he became increasingly convinced that it was going to be big. He was right. When "(Sittin' on) the Dock of the Bay" was released in January 1968, it went straight to the top of the Billboard charts, eventually selling more than two million copies. It was Otis Redding's biggest hit.

With a second verse that ends with, "Cause I've got nothing to live for, looks like nothing's gonna come my way," the song is not exactly a typical pop ballad. But to understand the success of this song, you have to understand the country to which it was released. Vietnam was in full swing, the civil rights movement was in its bloodiest chapter, and many felt just like that man on the dock: lonely, overwhelmed, and far from home. The song was a hit because it told the story of America in 1968.

Psychologists have long known that we gravitate toward the art, music, poetry, and literature that helps us make sense of the world and our part in it, especially during hard times. That's why everyone from the forlorn soldiers in Da Nang Province to self-medicated factory workers in Cleveland enjoyed seeing themselves sitting on the dock of that bay. They may not have been happy, but at least they weren't alone.

On December 10, 1967, Redding and his band boarded a small plane to fly from Cleveland to a show in Madison. When they were just four miles from the airport in Wisconsin, the plane had a mechanical failure and went down in Lake Monona. Everyone died except for the trumpet player, Ben Cauley. Redding would never see the success of his last and greatest song.

If you're trying to find meaning in the work you do, or the world in which you're doing it, close your eyes and imagine that you are sitting on that houseboat in Sausalito, California, watching the ferries cross the bay. When you look to your left, you see a 26-year-old Otis Redding writing the song of his generation. He stops playing, looks up at you, and asks, "What's your song about?"

What are you going to say?

The Shoeless Resilience

ON JULY 14, 1912, AMERICAN JIM THORPE was preparing for his second-to-last day of Olympic competition in Stockholm, Sweden. He had already won gold in the pentathlon the week before and he was leading in the decathlon that day. With less than 10 minutes to go before the high jump, Thorpe reached into his bag for his shoes... and kept reaching.

They were gone. Thorpe asked his teammates for an extra pair, but he received only one shoe. Too small. He put it on anyway and ran to a nearby trash can where he found a too-big shoe that he made fit by putting on two pairs of socks.

Thorpe competed in all of the remaining decathlon events that day with these mismatched shoes. He won another gold medal and set a 1,500-meter record that stood for 60 years.[87] This is what resilience looks like, and it's not surprising that Jim Thorpe had it. As an orphan who grew up poor in the Dust Bowl, he was the first Native American to compete in the Olympic Games. And nothing was going to stop Thorpe from winning that day.

The most creative, resourceful, and resilient thing on this planet is a human fueled by meaning. Fully aware of who they are, and what they are there to do. It's Kurt Vonnegut leaving his job at General Electric to write, Wilma Rudolph winning three gold medals after surviving Polio, and Katsusuke Yanagisawa taking that first step to climb Mount Everest at the age of 71. Powerful legacies to remind us of at least one thing.

If the shoe doesn't fit, wear it.

The Stories We Tell Ourselves

CHARLES DICKENS NEEDED MONEY. Sure, *Oliver Twist* and *The Old Curiosity Shop* had made him very famous, but his most recent series, *Martin Chuzzlewit*, had flopped spectacularly. With bills mounting and a fifth child on the way, his publisher decreased his pay. It was October 1843, and the situation was bleak.

Dickens wasn't alone. It was the so-called Hungry Forties, a period of depression and unemployment in England. Dickens had spent the previous months touring schools for street children to try to help them avoid a life of prison, pickpockets, sweatshop labor, and early death. And he was planning to write a short book called *An Appeal to the People of England on Behalf of the Poor Man's Child*, but now there was no time for that.

Dickens sat down to write a new book, and fast. Even though his publisher wouldn't support the project, he knew that if he could finish a book in two months or less, he might have a chance to self-publish and sell it as a Christmas gift. He worked long days and late nights, borrowed money to pay for the printing, and six weeks later he emerged with *A Christmas Carol*.[88]

It was his biggest hit. An instant bestseller that established Dickens as England's most famous living author, and the man who invented Christmas as we know it today. Initially, Dickens didn't make that much money from A Christmas Carol, as he insisted that each book be adorned with gold lettering on the cover and spine, gilded edges on every page, hand-colored illustrations, and four woodcuts by John Leech, all of which dwindled his initial profits to a mere £137.

Bah humbug, indeed. But *A Christmas Carol* was so much bigger than a bank account for Dickens. Because writing this book reconnected him with the one thing that success had taken away: his voice and purpose to serve the poor. It's reported that Dickens "wept over it, laughed, and wept again," and that he often walked 15 to 20 miles through the streets of London late at night just to reflect on this book.

If you asked Dickens what he was doing in October 1843, he would have said he was writing a Christmas book to make money for his family. But if you asked him after the book was done, he would have told you that he was using his words to serve the poor. And that renewed purpose fueled his late-life success. That is, Dickens wrote the story that transformed Dickens.

In this way, Dickens was ahead of his time. Psychologists have since articulated a concept called narrative identity, which is basically the idea that we become the stories we tell ourselves. The theory is best encapsulated by John Holmes, a psychology professor at University of Waterloo, who wrote: "Storytelling isn't just how we construct our identities; stories are our identities." That's why Dickens no longer felt like a downtrodden and desperate man after he wrote *A Christmas Carol*, even though he didn't initially make that much money from it. The act of writing it changed the story that he told himself about himself, and that was more powerful than any paycheck.

Which brings us to the last chapter. On March 15, 1870, Charles Dickens took the stage at St. James's Hall in London. He was there to read *A Christmas Carol*, by then his most-cherished work. At the end of the performance he said, "From these garish lights, I vanish now for evermore, with a heartfelt, grateful, respectful, and affectionate farewell."[89] With tears streaming down his face, Dickens raised his hands to his lips to send an affectionate kiss. He died three months later, but his final lesson never will.

The most important stories are the ones we tell ourselves.

V. **LEGACY**

"You blows who you is."

—Louis Armstrong

The Looking-Glass Self

EARLY IN WORLD WAR II, THE U.S. Army had no way to track how many planes it had, where planes were located, how many pilots were at each base, or what parts were needed. The logistics system was a guessing game, and the inefficiency started to take its toll. Seeing this, a group of 10 Army Air Force soldiers who called themselves the Whiz Kids devised a system using teletype machines and punch card calculators to generate daily logistics reports. In an era before computers, this system gave the U.S. a competitive advantage and ended up saving over $1 billion.

After the war, the Whiz Kids stuck together. They sent brochures to 100 major corporations to apply for work as a team, but they only got one response—from Henry Ford. He invited the team to Detroit and hired them all that day. The Whiz Kids rose quickly. Most became executives, and Robert McNamara even rose to be the first non-Ford president of the company.

Jack Reith became the president of Mercury. Reith had long dreamed of building the greatest American automobile. He worked obsessively to design it, micromanaging everything down to the shapes of the headlights, knobs, and door pulls. He called it the 1957 Mercury Turnpike Cruiser. With automatic adjusting "seat-o-matic" seats, a retractable rear window, and gold anodized trim, the car was the epitome of American excess. The ads called the car a "Preview of the Future," and Reith saw it as his greatest contribution to this country.[90]

Unfortunately, America didn't agree. Despite a national promotional tour, the car was met with abysmal sales—an unequivocal failure. The company discontinued the Cruiser in 1958, and Reith lost his job as the head of Mercury. He spiraled into a brutal and deep depression.

Jack Reith was ahead of his time. Not in the cars that he created, but in what motivated him to create them. Reith outsourced his self-esteem. He looked to customers, coworkers, and close relationships to give him the feedback that would help him define and build his own self-worth—a dangerous path.

To be fair, we are social creatures with instinctual needs for external validation from the people closest to us. The sociologist Charles Cooley wrote about this in his 1902 book, *Human Nature and the Social Order*. In that book he developed the now-famous concept of the looking-glass self, which he summarized as follows: "I am not what I think I am and I am not what you think I am; I am what I think that you think I am."[91]

Outsourcing our self-esteem appears to be on the rise today. In one recent survey, over 62 percent of people responded that their self-worth was strongly tied to what others think.[92] There is not a lot of research on what might be driving this trend, but two factors are likely at play in workplaces today.

1. **Social media is changing our brains**. Much has been written about how the real-time validation that is engineered into social media triggers dopamine-driven feedback loops that make the platforms addictive. It's why adults in America average two to four hours per day tapping and typing on their devices, adding up to more than 2,600 daily touches.[93] But that addiction doesn't necessarily stop with our phones. Once we train our brains to prioritize external validation, we will seek it at work in meetings, email threads, product launches, and more. It becomes a bucket that never fills.

2. **Modern work can be shallow**. In his book, *Deep Work*, Cal Newport paints a picture of work today where we face an endless stream of emails, meetings, and logistical work. By completing these transactional tasks, we can trigger a quick sense of accomplishment and external validation. And just like those social media posts, these logistical tasks can become addictive. But shallow work doesn't actually contribute significant long-term value to ourselves or the organization.

So, what can we do? In his book, *21 Lessons for the 21st Century*, Yuval Noah Harari argues that the most important thing we can do to survive in a world with increasing change and uncertainty is discover the power of self-reflection and non-attachment using meditation. Put simply, the self-worth we need for the future will come from within, by detaching ourselves from the things that we cannot control, including the looking-glass self.

If only Reith had realized it. At 2 a.m. on July 3, 1960, he grabbed a .38 caliber Colt revolver and shot himself twice in the chest. It was his son's seventh birthday. His is the tragic story of a man with seemingly infinite ambition, vision, and creativity who just couldn't see past the looking-glass self.

To Jack Reith, and the peace inside us all.

Your Story Will Expire

IN 1985, ISRAEL MACALLISTER BOOTH sat down to write a letter to the shareholders of the Polaroid Corporation. Despite decreasing demand for instant cameras, Polaroid was still a very successful company. And they were about to release the most advanced instant camera ever made: The Polaroid Spectra, complete with automatic focusing and a self-timer.

It's why MacAllister Booth, as CEO, confidently wrote this to shareholders[94]:

> *"As electronic imaging becomes more prevalent, there remains a basic human need for a permanent*

> *visual record. Whether that record fulfills an emotional requisite in the visual diaries of amateur photography or provides practical data in an industrial or scientific setting, the universal insatiable appetite for visual communication and portable information will be constant, reflecting a continuing need for instantly available, high-quality print media."*

In short, don't worry about digital; we got this. Of course, we know now that they did not have it. That letter, and the assumptions it contained, turned out to be false. Sales continued to decline, and the company filed for bankruptcy in 2001. More than 21,000 Polaroid jobs were lost.

Companies are more likely to fail today than at any point in history. Toys R Us, JCPenney, Neiman Marcus, Sears, and others have all suffered similar fates. We could talk all day about why this is, about how hard it is for organizations to navigate a global pandemic and other external forces like disruptive technology, globalization, and regulation, but that probably wouldn't be entirely productive. Too many of those conversations will land us in a place where we repeat platitudes like, "The only constant in life is change."

Unfortunately, platitudes don't help us avoid Polaroid's fate. In order to really understand how organizations might adapt more quickly, we need to remember this: Your story will expire.

Every person goes through a series of distinct phases in life. And in each phase, we define our identities with a story. For example, I might say that I am a varsity football player who gets good grades. But when we move to the next phase in life, those old stories expire. So, when that varsity football player goes to college and doesn't make the team, he has to define a new story. Nobody really cares about the games he won in high school.

The same is true for organizations. The scrappy startup scales, and its underdog story no longer fits. The market leader gets disrupted, but it continues to hold on to its success in the past. Real growth requires us to detach from old stories to write the next.

But the stories we tell about ourselves don't die easily. It takes a lot of self-awareness to even see the inflection points in life—the moments where we are becoming something new. But if you miss those moments, you risk believing Polaroid's success is guaranteed because instant photographs will always fulfill an "emotional requisite in the visual diaries of amateur photography." Expired stories become expired truths.

As we stand here in the ashes of the RadioShacks, Kodaks, and Blockbusters of the world, it's important to remember that we are not the victims of circumstance. That we are not here just holding out hope for the best. We never have been.

Our stories may expire, but we don't have to.

The pen is in our hands.

A Man

GRAVES GET THE LAST WORD. Of all the words you utter, write, or sing in a lifetime, your headstone offers your last and most permanent chance to talk to the world. Charles Bukowski's reads, "Don't try." Rodney Dangerfield's says, "…there goes the neighborhood." But Charles L. "Sonny" Liston's fascinates me the most.

Liston knocked out Floyd Patterson in the first round to become the 1962 world heavyweight champion. The Ring magazine ranked him among the top 15 boxers of all time. Unfortunately, this isn't why most people know Liston.

His story was hard from the start. Born to sharecroppers in Arkansas during the Depression, Liston was the 24th of 25 children. He endured an alcoholic father, long days picking cotton, and perpetual poverty. Liston's parents forgot his birthday and middle name (both mysteries to this day), and he later reflected that, "The only thing I ever got from my old man was a beating."[95] His home wasn't a happy place.

So it's no surprise that Liston was arrested more than 20 times as a kid, eventually doing two years in the Missouri State Penitentiary for armed robbery. That's where he learned to fight. Liston defeated every opponent in the prison ring, which got him noticed by a local boxing promoter named Frank Mitchell. Mitchell pulled strings to get Liston paroled, a room at the Pine Street YMCA, and a job with a steel company in St. Louis.

For the first time maybe ever, Liston had someone on his side and a chance at redemption. He won the Golden Gloves championship and went professional less than a year later. Liston won 34 of 35 fights from 1953 to 1961, most by knockout. And despite being arrested another 14 times during those years, he got his title shot. Liston became the first man in history to knock out a champion in the first round, and he held the title for 17 months.

His reign ended in 1964. That's when a boisterous upstart named Cassius Clay got the chance to face the champ. In their first fight, Liston lost after refusing to start the seventh round, despite being equal in points. (He cited a shoulder injury.) The rematch was set for May 1965, and he lost that one too. A now-infamous "phantom punch" barely grazed Liston, yet somehow knocked him out in the first round. A fight fixed by Liston's mafia connections? Maybe. But a champion no more.

So began the sad decline of Sonny Liston. He died at home alone six years later from lung congestion and heart failure with heroin in his system. The end of his story, but for that last line—a two-word epitaph on a headstone that simply reads: "A MAN." It was written by his friend Mike Parkhurst, who said it summed up all of Liston's simplicity and contradictions. A stark reminder that we are more than the list of good and bad things we do, and that each of us might have some contradictions too.

We won't forget you, champ.

When the World Goes Quiet

I SWEAT THROUGH MY SHIRT ON THE walk from my spot in a distant lot to the nearest door of the Pentagon. It was July 2012, and such was life for an American bureaucrat in the height of humidity in Washington, D.C. Once in the building, I walked a quarter-mile to my cubicle on the fifth floor, set my stuff down, and took my French press coffee mug over to the water cooler to get 16 ounces of near-boiling water. With mug brewing, I sat down at my desk and logged in to the computer. This was my morning routine.

As I got settled in, I received a call on my desk line. I picked up the receiver, put it against my left ear, and said hello. But I didn't hear a clear response on the other end. Instead, I heard what sounded like a lo-fi 1920s recording coming through a blown speaker.

I was startled, but didn't think it was a big deal. I moved the receiver to my right ear where everything sounded fine. And for the next three weeks, I used my right ear when I needed to talk on the phone and said, "What's that?" a lot more than normal. The hearing in my left ear eventually came back, and I didn't think much about it.

That is, until it happened again in August 2013. Same scenario and same reaction. And again in July 2014. I didn't have a proper medical diagnosis, but after five years of losing my hearing in my left ear for a few weeks every summer, I grew to tolerate the temporary peace and quiet.

But everything changed last year. My hearing in the left ear disappeared right on cue, but this time I couldn't hear clearly in my right. It turns out that I have a non-cancerous growth inside my inner right ear that permanently damaged the hearing on that side. This left me unable to understand most voices, especially those in a higher frequency.

Now, I was scared. It's one thing to have to switch the phone to the other ear; it's another to be in a room with a group of friends who sound like they're speaking a foreign language you don't understand. Being in that room does something to you—or at least it did to me. I started to feel like a ghost, even with the people I love the most.

Because at some point you will get to a place where it's no longer practical to say, "What's that?" every time that you don't understand. So, you'll either politely smile and hope they don't know that you have no idea what is happening or risk joining the conversation that you thought you heard. Either way, these stilted interactions can create new friction and distance in your relationships.

And when my doctor told me that the hearing in my left ear may never come back, it became clear that there would be no ignoring this one. I got a hearing aid, which has significantly helped me understand the words that people say. Of course, the irony is that hearing aids also strip out the richness of sound, so the world now sounds like it's coming through an aging payphone on urban streets.

Needless to say, it's an adjustment.

At some point, we all come face-to-face with our human

frailty. The moment that you can't lift those boxes you used to, the day your vision fades and makes driving unsafe, or the pain that prevents you from walking long distances. In these instances, we can take comfort in the words offered by the inimitable David Bowie in a 1999 interview with the journalist Aaron Hicklin. When asked about the process of growing old, Bowie said, "I think ageing is an extraordinary process whereby you become the person that you always should have been."[96]

And that's just it, isn't it? When we lose our ability to move, hear, speak, or see, we are forced to detach from large parts of the outside world. And when that happens, we are given new perspective and the opportunity to ask ourselves life's biggest questions. Questions that connect us with a deeper sense of who we are. Questions that help us understand that when we lose our abilities, we can find ourselves.

The world may be a bit quieter now, but that one came through loud and clear.

A Book in the Pocket

SHORTLY AFTER COMING HOME from World War II, a soldier and his wife named their new daughter Betty Smith in honor of the author of *A Tree Grows in Brooklyn*. Afterward, the father wrote Smith a letter to say that every time they spoke their daughter's name, it would be in tribute to her.[97]

Another soldier wrote to Smith to say: "I can't explain the emotional reaction that took place, I only know that it happened and that this heart of mine turned over and became alive again. A surge of confidence has swept through me and I feel that maybe a fellow has a fighting chance in this world after all. I'll never be able to explain to you the gratitude and love that fill my heart in appreciation of what your book means to me."[98]

Smith received more than 10,000 letters like these.

It was no accident that so many soldiers read this book. Between 1943 and 1947, the United States military sent 123 million copies of more than 1,000 titles to troops serving overseas.[99] To make this possible, 70 different publishing companies coordinated to create paperbacks designed for America's service members: the Armed Services Edition. Sized to fit inside the hip or breast pocket of a military uniform, these miniature books included westerns, mysteries, comics, biographies, poetry, classics, and contemporary fiction.

In part, this was an initiative to give soldiers some solace from the sustained boredom and pain that comes with war. But it was also a defiant stand against the censorship taking place in Germany, a country where Nazis burned more than 100 million books and destroyed hundreds of libraries, institutes, and rare book collections. One American wartime poster featuring a quote from Franklin D. Roosevelt captures the sentiment best:

> *"Books cannot be killed by fire. People die, but books never die. No man and no force can put thought in a concentration camp forever. No man and no force can take from the world the books that embody man's eternal fight against tyranny. In this war, we know, books are weapons. Books are weapons in the war of ideas."*

While these books were effective in spreading ideas, their most powerful quality was the ability to transform readers. Consider *A Tree Grows in Brooklyn*, which tells the coming-of-age story of a young girl named Francie Nolan. Her impoverished family scraped by on her mother's wages from cleaning houses and the occasional contribution from her alcoholic dad. It was a hard life, but Nolan escaped the suffering that surrounded her with books and a dream of going to college one day. When her dad died, she had to quit school to take a job to support the family—but Nolan didn't let her dream die with him. She studied at all hours, eventually passing the college entrance exams to get into the University of Michigan. A dream realized.

Throughout it all, there was a tree growing from the sidewalk outside of her apartment in Williamsburg. A tree that wouldn't die, even though it had been cut down, burned, and deprived of basically all nutrients and plant necessities. It was that tree that gave Nolan the will to not just survive the hard times, but to find a way to thrive.

The best stories are contagious.

When those soldiers read about the impossible odds facing Nolan, they saw themselves in her. What was a third-person story slowly shifted to the first, and Nolan's ending eventually became theirs. Finding ourselves in the stories we read can help us through the hardest times. Holden Caulfield keeps me from feeling alone, Rosa Parks brings me resolve, Atticus Finch teaches me compassion, and Tom Joad provides me a moral compass for the long road.

The best stories are contagious because when we see ourselves in them, we also see a path forward. As we embark on another run of hard times, maybe it's time to find those stories again.

There's a book waiting for you right now.

The Evolution of Success

ON A FERRY RIDE TO SAN FRANCISCO, Martin Eden looked over to see a rowdy group of drunk young men beating up a stranger. Guided by his profound sense of street justice, Eden jumped into the fray, knocked out a few teeth, and single-handedly fought off all of the attackers. The grateful victim, a man named Arthur Morse, invited Eden over for dinner to thank him. It was a dinner that he would never forget.

Martin Eden was a sailor. True to the legacy of hard-living seafarers of the early 1900s, he had no education, no money, and a body full of scars to prove it. Morse, on the other hand, was well-educated and quite wealthy. When Eden arrived at the house for dinner in his ragged suit, he couldn't imagine a more intimidating scene. Then he saw the oil painting on the wall.

Depicting a small sailboat up against a heavy surf with storm clouds overhead, Eden couldn't believe the intricate details captured by the artist, right down to the grain of the wood on the deck. From there, he saw a pile of books on the table. He randomly picked one up by the English poet Algernon Charles Swinburne and started feverishly reading. Eden was intoxicated, and for the first time in his life, it wasn't from the drink.

As he devoured Swinburne, he heard Morse say, "Ruth, this is Mr. Eden."[100] Eden looked up and saw her. The paintings, books, and music were one thing, but this girl was something else entirely. Her smooth skin, blue eyes, and angel face transported him to another place. She wanted to meet the man who saved her brother's life. The two sat down to talk, and even though they came from completely different worlds, they both felt an undeniable spark.

Later reflecting on this night, Eden said that he felt like a starving man finding food for the first time. He knew he couldn't go back to his brutish life on the sea. So, over the course of the next three years, he worked hard jobs during the day and immersed himself in books at night. It was no easy road, but it did help Eden find his true calling. He was going to be a writer.

His vision was clear: Get stories published in magazines, write a book, find great success, and earn the status and wealth that he needed to marry Ruth Morse. And while he knew that other people may have more talent, he was sure that no one had more grit. Eden worked long hours in a laundry to save money, then took time off to write and send manuscripts to magazines. He lived this cycle for three years until he had a stack of rejections as high as his desk. Three years of "no" took its toll.

Toward the end of this stretch, Eden pawned his coat, then his watch, and finally his bicycle. He was only eating one potato per day and on the brink of starvation. With Ruth Morse long gone, he was just about to give up when he got an offer from a magazine to buy his manuscript for five dollars. An offer that was followed by a neverending cascade of acceptances from magazines.

He received more money in the year that followed than he could have dreamed. The publishers who used to ignore or reject him now desperately sought the very same manuscripts they had mailed back the year before. There were book offers, speaking requests, endless accolades, and renewed admiration from Ruth Morse. Eden sat firmly atop the high society that he worked so hard to join. He had arrived—yet he felt empty inside.

Eden couldn't get past the fact that nothing in his work had changed from the days when he was broke, alone, and rejected. He wanted the world to love his work because it moved them, not because it was trendy or profitable to do so. Eden felt duped. So he gave away much of his wealth to friends and family and booked a porthole cabin on the SS Mariposa to Tahiti. Fair winds and following seas.

Eden found little peace on that boat. Each day of the journey left him more depressed. One night when he couldn't sleep, he turned on the bedside light and flipped open a book to a poem by Swinburne:

> *From too much love of living,*
>   *From hope and fear set free,*
> *We thank with brief thanksgiving*
>   *Whatever gods may be*
> *That no life lives forever;*
> *That dead men rise up never;*
> *That even the weariest river*
>   *Winds somewhere safe to sea.*

That dead men rise up never. For the first time that he could remember, Eden saw a path to peace. He opened the porthole and looked down at the seemingly infinite depths beneath him. Eden took one more look at his physical world, inhaled a deep breath, and dove to a depth from which he would never return. Even the weariest river winds somewhere safe to sea.

This is not a true story.

Well, not entirely. *Martin Eden* is a 1909 novel written by Jack London at the height of his success. (In fact, he wanted to call this book *Success*.[101]) And given that London was also a sailor who worked for three years to teach himself how to write, *Martin Eden* is undoubtedly based on his own life. Also like Eden, London felt that his success was somewhat arbitrary and empty.

But there is a critical difference between the two men. Jack London didn't write this book because he saw himself in Martin Eden; he wrote it because he was worried that the rest of the world did. This book was London's plea to save men and women from the emptiness that he saw in rampant individualism. Because London believed that if we only focus on our own achievements and ignore the needs of others, we will never find the peace we seek.

What if London was right? In his 2015 book *The Road to Character*, David Brooks wrote about a study published in 1954. Psychologists asked more than 10,000 adolescents whether they considered themselves to be a very important person. At that point, just 12 percent said yes. The same study was replicated in 1989, and this time roughly 80 percent said yes. Did we all get more important, or did we forget about each other?

With addiction and depression on the rise, there are too many of us who feel like Eden on the Mariposa. Looking down from the porthole to infinite depths, hungry to be something more than we are today. But maybe we can pull ourselves back, close that hatch, and remember that the road to success is never walked alone. The dead men may rise up never, but we can when we're together.

You are not alone.

CONCLUSION

JANIS JOPLIN STOOD AT AN unmarked grave in the Mount Lawn Cemetery in Philadelphia on August 7, 1970. She was there to pay tribute to one of the musicians who inspired her the most: Bessie Smith. With an uncanny ability to sing songs that gave voice to life's hardest, and most universal, truths, Smith earned unprecedented fame and recognition in the 1920s. She sold more than six million records, and became the highest paid black entertainer in America.[102] It's why Smith is considered the "Empress of the Blues."

Her work would shape the future of music, with Aretha Franklin, Louis Armstrong, Billie Holiday, Queen Latifah, and many more citing Smith as a pivotal influence and inspiration. While her legacy may live long, her life was cut short at age 43. On September 26, 1937, Smith died after the car she was in collided with a truck on Route 61 between Memphis, Tennessee, and Clarksdale, Mississippi.[103] Despite the fact that thousands of people came to her funeral, Bessie Smith was buried in an unmarked grave.

Until that day in August 1970. Janis Joplin and a nurse named Juanita Green bought a marble headstone for Bessie Smith, and they were joined by 50 others to watch as it was installed. Jazz historian John Hammon wrote the epitaph: "The greatest blues singer in the world will never stop singing."

A long overdue tribute to one of the most influential

voices in history.

I love the idea that Bessie Smith is still singing today. Her songs galvanized a generation of people whose work inspired the next. It's a part of the chain of influence and inspiration that has fueled our development as a species, whether in music, art, science, technology, business, health, or society. Each generation sings the songs of the last before they can write their own.

And that's really what this book is all about. Those old work songs taught the next generation the lessons they needed to do the work they do. Lessons that could support, strengthen, inspire, heal, teach, and give meaning. But when we let those songs die, we broke the chain. We disconnected ourselves from the generations of workers whose words and songs we need the most.

So, even though we face a future enticing us with promises of technology and progress, we must remember to look backward—to hear the stories of the generations that came before us. We need to sing their songs before we can write our own.

Two short months after buying Bessie Smith's headstone, Janis Joplin would get her own. She died in room 105 at the Landmark Motor Hotel on October 4, 1970. Her final and most popular record, *Pearl*, was released posthumously in January 1971.

Thank god we have her songs to sing, because they might just help us write our own.

To the songs inside us all.

ACKNOWLEDGEMENTS

I SAID THIS FOR THE LAST BOOK, but must say it again. No book is published alone. It takes a team. Sometimes that team comes from a corporation with publishing professionals working for a better product to grow the bottom line, and that's fine. But sometimes it's not that at all. Sometimes it's a group of people who take a dream and make it real. A group of incredible people. That's my team, and it's not hyperbole. This book would not exist without the people listed below.

First and foremost, thank you Angie Cooper. You are a legendary soul, and I am so grateful to share this life with you. You have supported and inspired me beyond what I thought was possible, and you changed the way I see the world. Thank you.

To my editor, Katherine Schutt, you are so incredibly talented, and your work helped me to not just improve this book, but to reimagine the way I write. If this book were an album, you'd be my Rick Rubin, and I'll never forget what you did here.

To Max Kuhn, you are the artist of a generation. Your paintings tell stories better than any words I'll ever write, and your work with this cover took my breath away. Thank you.

To Brad Clifford, thank you for your incredible work with the layout and related shirt design (and for the many important songs that you've written). Madison Johnson, thank you for your support with the typeset, and for still picking up the phone when I call with whacky one-off design projects.

Mom and Dad, thank you for always supporting me and for letting me learn how to tell stories from you. To my sister Megan, you're way funnier than me, which I only resent a little, but I love you and I forgive you for smashing a tennis racquet over my head.

Of course, the list doesn't end there. There are many of you who played a role in this book who may not even know it. Christian Golden, thank you for helping me push these ideas to a more sophisticated and nuanced place. Adrian McCavitt, you have endured so many half-baked versions of these stories, thanks always for your support and deep insights into our nature as people. Naomi McCavitt, I have thoroughly enjoyed discussing the creative process with you, and I have learned so much from the way you see and do your work.

To Mike Kvidera, Seth Campbell, Paul Hoeppner, Matt Moody, Mark Anthoney, Chris Buroughs, Jason Humphreys, Scott Christie, Peter Sawyer, John Pace, Dave Byrd, and anyone else I played music with, thank you for helping me discover the rhythm of writing.

And so much gratitude to a host of other loved ones, including Steve Crandall for the inspiration, Robby Smolen for the endless stoke, Tad Peyton, Rachel Corbett, Dean Hurley, RJ and Alicia, Dawn Pace, Nick Wurz, Andrew Everding, Will Renton, Jonathan Fuller, Kyle Hurley,

Bryan Buchanan, Bird Cox, David Phinney, Grace Kuhn, Kate Duffy, Ryan Mauter, Darren Brown, Clay Cutchins, TayRex, Kevin Wilson, Aaron McClung, Scott Wayne, Aaron O'Dell, Jamie and Kristin Hedges, Corryne Graf, Emily Hardesty, Joe Slonecker, Josh Smith, Sara Burns, Thomas Behne, Adam Schmidt, Tim Gillespie, Chris Cee, John Music, Kelly Segura, Jabeen Akhtar, Rowan Hildreth, Kyle and Margaret Hurley, Ray Harkins, Sidney Brown, Sari Wiener, Mike Schleibaum, Brian Speer, Matty Green, Maha Shami, and Matt Michel.

ENDNOTES

1 Bernard Weinraub, "An Ex-Convict, a Hit Album, An Ending Fit for Hollywood," *New York Times*, March 3, 2002, https://www.nytimes.com/2002/03/03/us/an-ex-convict-a-hit-album-an-ending-fit-for-hollywood.html.

2 Dennis McLellan, "James Carter, 77; Singer in Chain Gang Found Fame," *Los Angeles Times*, December 8, 2003, https://www.latimes.com/archives/la-xpm-2003-dec-08-me-carter8-story.html.

3 Paul Trachtman, "Matisse & Picasso," *Smithsonian Magazine*, February 2003, https://www.smithsonianmag.com/arts-culture/matisse-picasso-75440861.

4 Janet Flanner, "Pablo Picasso's Idiosyncratic Genius A life in art," *New Yorker*, March 9, 1957, https://www.newyorker.com/magazine/1957/03/09/the-surprise-of-the-century-i.

5 Fisun Güner, "How a small African figurine changed art," *BBC*, August 21, 2017, http://www.bbc.com/culture/story/20170818-how-a-small-african-figurine-changed-art.

6 Robert Rosenthal and Lenore Jacobson, "Teachers' Expectancies: Determinants of Pupils' IQ Gains," *Psychological Reports*, 19, (August 1966): 115–118.

7 Lawrence Wright, *The Looming Tower: Al-Qaeda and the Road to 9/11* (New York: Vintage Books, 2006).

8 Yuval Harari, *Sapiens: A Brief History of Humankind* (New York: HarperCollins, 2015).

9 "Stories," Harper Collins, accessed April 12, 2020, https://200.hc.com/stories/the-harper-fire-of-1853.

10 Megan Garber, "'It Repels the Reader': Tech Glitches Led Moby-Dick's First Critics to Pan It," *The Atlantic*, November 13, 2015, https://www.theatlantic.com/technology/archive/2013/11/it-repels-the-reader-tech-glitches-led-i-moby-dick-i-s-first-critics-to-pan-it/281499.

11 Nathaniel Philbrick, "The Road to Melville," *Vanity Fair*, October 20, 2011, https://www.vanityfair.com/culture/2011/11/moby-dick-201111.

12 Tina Jordan, "'Abnormal, as Most Geniuses Are': Celebrating 200 Years of Herman Melville," *New York Times*, August 1, 2019, https://www.nytimes.com/2019/08/01/books/herman-melville-moby-dick.html.

13 Charles Babington, "Baltimore's role in reviving Herman Melville (and his whale of a tale)," *Baltimore Sun*, July 26, 2019, https://www.baltimoresun.com/opinion/op-ed/bs-ed-op-0728-melville-baltimore-20190726-7o4yuxnmujg4zmotjrawwkxmny-story.html.

14 Joseph Campbell, "Joseph Campbell and the Power of Myth — 'The First Storytellers,'" interview by Bill Moyers, *PBS*, June 23, 1988, video, 2:16, https://billmoyers.com/content/ep-3-joseph-campbell-and-the-power-of-myth-the-first-storytellers-audio.

15 Hannah Keyser, "The Story That Launched Nellie Bly's Famed Journalism Career," *Mental Floss*, May 5, 2015, https://www.mentalfloss.com/article/63759/story-launched-nellie-blys-famed-journalism-career.

16 The name came from an old folk song written by Stephen Foster, who also wrote "Oh! Susanna" and "Camptown Races."

17 Christopher Klein, "Nellie Bly's Biggest Scoops," *History.com*, August 22, 2018, https://www.history.com/news/nellie-blys-biggest-scoops.

18 Klein, "Nellie Bly's Biggest Scoops."

19 Angie Martoccio, "Tom Petty's 'Wildflowers': 10 Things You Didn't Know," *Rolling Stone*, November 1, 2019, https://www.rollingstone.com/music/music-features/tom-petty-wildflowers-things-you-didnt-know-904098.

20 Malcolm Gladwell, interview with Rick Rubin, *Broken Record*, podcast audio, December 24, 2018, https://brokenrecordpodcast.com/episode-7-tom-petty-and-the-creation-of-wildflowers.

21 In October 2020, Tom Petty's wife, Dana, and his daughters coordinated with Rubin and the band to release the songs as part of a *Wildflowers* box set.

22 Patti Smith, *M Train* (New York: Vintage Books, 2015), 202.

23 Malcolm Gladwell, interview with Rick Rubin, *Broken Record*, podcast audio, December 24, 2018, https://brokenrecordpodcast.com/episode-7-tom-petty-and-the-creation-of-wildflowers.

24 Charlotte Zoë Walker, *Sharp Eyes: John Burroughs and American Nature Writing* (New York: Syracuse University Press, 2000).

25 America's National Parks Podcast, *A Strenuous Holiday*, podcast audio, August 31, 2018, https://nationalparkpodcast.com/a-strenuous-holiday.

26 Steven Pearlstein, "How the cult of shareholder value wrecked American business," *Washington Post*, September 9, 2013, https://www.washingtonpost.com/news/wonk/wp/2013/09/09/how-the-cult-of-shareholder-value-wrecked-american-business.

27 "Digital Collections," The Henry Ford, accessed April 12, 2020, https://www.thehenryford.org/collections-and-research/digital-collections/artifact/225212.

28 Rodney Mullen, "On getting up again," filmed October 2013 at TEDxOrangeCoast, Costa Mesa, CA, video, 18:36, https://www.youtube.com/watch?v=DBbmNAZWq-E.

29 Ed Andrews, "Rodney Mullen, Another Dimension," *Huck Magazine*, April 15, 2010, https://www.huckmag.com/outdoor/skate/rodney-mullen.

30 Steve Turner, *Jack Kerouac: Angelheaded Hipster* (New York: Viking, 1996), 117.

31 Mullen, "On getting up again."

32 Paul Avrich, *An American Anarchist: The Life of Voltairine de Cleyre* (Princeton: Princeton University Press, 1978), 63.

33 History.com Editors, "Haymarket Riot," History.com, October 9, 2019, https://www.history.com/topics/19th-century/haymarket-riot.

34 History.com Editors, "Gilded Age," *History.com*, February 13, 2018, https://www.history.com/topics/19th-century/gilded-age.

35 William C. Gannett, *Blessed Be Drudgery And A Cup Of Cold Water* (Washington: Review and Herald, 1914), 27.

36 Viktor Frankl, *Man's Search for Meaning* (Boston: Beacon Press, 1959).

37 Hardeep Phull, "Secrets behind 'Born in the USA' as Bruce Springsteen's classic turns 35," *New York Post*, July 3, 2019, https://nypost.com/2019/07/03/secrets-behind-born-in-the-usa-as-bruce-springsteens-classic-turns-35.

38 Dave Marsh, *Glory Days* (New York: Pantheon, 1987), 229.

39 Lester Coch and John French, "Overcoming Resistance to Change," *Human Relations 1*, (1948).

40 Teresa Amabile and Steven J. Kramer, "The Power of Small Wins," *Harvard Business Review*, May 2011, https://hbr.org/2011/05/the-power-of-small-wins.

41 William Lonsdale Watkinson, *The supreme conquest, and other sermons preached in America* (New York: F.H. Revell company, 1907), 219.

42 Dashiell Coleman, "1929 strike: Ella May, mother and activist, slain," *Gaston Gazette*, April 27, 2019, https://www.gastongazette.com/news/20190427/1929-strike-ella-may-mother-and-activist-slain.

43 Annette Cox, "The Saga of Ella May Wiggins," *Southern Cultures* 21, no. 3 (Fall 2015): 111-115.

44 Peter Waldman and Kartikay Mehrota, "America's Worst Graveyard Shift Is Grinding Up Workers," *Bloomberg Businessweek*, December 29, 2017, https://www.bloomberg.com/news/features/2017-12-29/america-s-worst-graveyard-shift-is-grinding-up-workers

45 Andrew Wasley, Christopher Cook, and Natalie Jones, "Two Amputations a Week: The Cost of Working in a US Meat Plant," *The Guardian*, July 5, 2018, https://www.theguardian.com/environment/2018/jul/05/amputations-serious-injuries-us-meat-industry-plant.

46 Michael Harris, "Why the Proof of Fermat's Last Theorem Doesn't Need to Be Enhanced," *Quanta Magazine*, June 3, 2019, https://www.quantamagazine.org/why-the-proof-of-fermats-last-theorem-doesnt-need-to-be-enhanced-20190603.

47 John O'Connor and Edmund Robertson, "MacTutor History of Mathematics Archive," *University of St Andrews, Scotland*, September 2009, https://www-history.mcs.st-andrews.ac.uk/Biographies/Wiles.html.

48 PBS, "The Proof," *NOVA*, October 28, 1997, https://www.pbs.org/wgbh/nova/transcripts/2414proof.html.

49 PBS, "The Proof."

50 Helen O'Neill, "Experts Say You Have to be a Little Crazy," *The Hartford Courant*, October 15, 1995, https://www.courant.com/news/connecticut/hc-xpm-1995-10-15-9510130051-story.html

51 There were issues with the proof discovered during the peer review process, so Wiles had to spend the following two years fixing his work. However, by 1995 his work was done, and Fermat's Last Theorem was officially solved.

52 Scott Bronstein, Curt Devine, and Drew Griffin, "He's Accused of War Crimes and Torture. Uber and Lyft Approved Him to Drive," *CNN*, May 15, 2019, https://edition.cnn.com/2019/05/14/business/uber-driver-accused-war-criminal-invs/index.html.

53. David Stout, "Ex-Somali Army Officer Is Arrested in Virginia," *New York Times*, February 28, 1998, https://www.nytimes.com/1998/02/28/world/ex-somali-army-officer-is-arrested-in-virginia.html.

54. Conor Gaffey, "General Butt Naked and Other Former Warlords Roam Free in Liberia. Will a New President Prosecute Them?," *Newsweek*, November 8, 2017, https://www.newsweek.com/liberia-war-general-butt-naked-ellen-johnson-sirleaf-701232.

55. Erving Goffman, *The Presentation of Self in Everyday Life* (New York: Doubleday, 1959).

56. Evan Niu, "Nokia Could Have Beat the iPhone to Market," *The Motley Fool*, July 20, 2012, https://www.fool.com/investing/general/2012/07/20/nokia-could-have-beat-the-iphone-to-market.aspx.

57. Robert Axelrod, *The Evolution of Cooperation* (Cambridge, MA: Basic Books, 1984).

58. Charles Duhigg, "What Google Learned From Its Quest to Build the Perfect Team," *New York Times*, February 25, 2016, https://www.nytimes.com/2016/02/28/magazine/what-google-learned-from-its-quest-to-build-the-perfect-team.html.

59. Dina Newman, "Alexei Stakhanov: The USSR's superstar miner," *BBC*, December 30, 2015, https://www.bbc.com/news/magazine-35161610.

60. Newman, "Alexei Stakhanov: The USSR's superstar miner."

61. Theodore Shabad, "Stakhanov, a Soviet Miner, Is Dead; Name Was Byword for Hard Work," *New York Times*, November 6, 1977, https://www.nytimes.com/1977/11/06/archives/stakhanov-a-soviet-miner-is-dead-name-was-byword-for-hard-work.html.

62. Serge Schmemann, "In Soviet, Eager Beaver's Legend Works Overtime," *New York Times*, August 31, 1985, https://www.nytimes.com/1985/08/31/world/in-soviet-eager-beaver-s-legend-works-overtime.html.

63 Oliver Burkeman, "Why time management is ruining our lives," *The Guardian*, December 22, 2016, https://www.theguardian.com/technology/2016/dec/22/why-time-management-is-ruining-our-lives.

64 Mark Connelly, *George Orwell: A Literary Companion* (North Carolina: McFarland & Company, 2018), 47.

65 Newman, "Alexei Stakhanov: The USSR's superstar miner."

66 Matthew Clavin, *Toussaint Louverture and the American Civil War: The Promise and Peril of a Second Haitian Revolution* (Pittsburgh: University of Pennsylvania Press, 2012).

67 Cyril Lionel Robert James, *The Black Jacobins* (New York: Vintage Books, 1963).

68 Madison Smartt Bell, "Books: Rebel Rebel," *The New Republic*, September 10, 2007, https://newrepublic.com/article/63613/books-rebel-rebel.

69 Owen Edwards, "A Larger-Than-Life Toussaint Louverture," *Smithsonian Magazine*, May 2011, https://www.smithsonianmag.com/arts-culture/a-larger-than-life-toussaint-louverture-1651712.

70 Jim Clifton, "How DTE Energy Emerged Stronger After the Great Recession," *Gallup*, December 13, 2017, https://news.gallup.com/opinion/chairman/223316/dte-energy-emerged-stronger-great-recession.aspx.

71 Clifton, "How DTE Energy Emerged Stronger After the Great Recession."

72 Tony Perry, "Marines' 'Mad Dog Mattis' Battles for Iraqis' Support," *Los Angeles Times*, April 16, 2004, https://www.latimes.com/archives/la-xpm-2004-apr-16-fg-general16-story.html.

73 Martin Chilton, "Kind of Blue: The jazz album by Miles Davis that transformed music," *Independent*, March 1, 2019, https://www.independent.co.uk/arts-entertainment/music/features/miles-davis-kind-of-blue-jazz-album-a8799061.html.

74 Jerome Maunsell, "It's just too good to be blue," *The Guardian*, March 17, 2001, https://www.theguardian.com/theobserver/2001/mar/18/music.

75 Miles Davis with Quincy Troupe, *Miles Davis: The Autobiography* (New York: Simon & Schuster, 1989).

76 Peter Dizikes, "A new approach to diversity research," *MIT News*, June 4, 2014, http://news.mit.edu/2014/new-approach-diversity-research-0604.

77 Addison Nugent, "When Miles Davis and John Coltrane Scandalized Paris," *Ozy.com*, March 22, 2018, https://www.ozy.com/flashback/when-miles-davis-and-john-coltrane-scandalized-paris/85361.

78 James Hale, "Miles Davis & John Coltrane: Display of Different Minds," *Downbeat*, June 20, 2018, http://downbeat.com/news/detail/miles-davis-john-coltrane-display-of-different-minds.

79 Jim Harter, "Employee Engagement on the Rise in the U.S.," *Gallup*, August 26, 2018, https://news.gallup.com/poll/241649/employee-engagement-rise.aspx.

80 Paul Raffaele, "In John They Trust," *Smithsonian Magazine*, February 2006, https://www.smithsonianmag.com/history/in-john-they-trust-109294882.

81 Yves Morieux, "Smart Rules: Six Ways to Get People to Solve Problems Without You," *Harvard Business Review*, September 2011, https://hbr.org/2011/09/smart-rules-six-ways-to-get-people-to-solve-problems-without-you.

82 IBM Institute for Business Value, "Capitalizing on Complexity," *Global Chief Executive Officer Study*, May 2010, https://www.ibm.com/downloads/cas/1VZV5X8J.

83 Dimple Agarwal, Ardie van Berkel, and Burt Rea, "Simplification of Work: The Coming Revolution," *Deloitte Insights*, February 27, 2015, https://www2.deloitte.com/us/en/insights/focus/human-capital-trends/2015/work-simplification-human-capital-trends-2015.html.

84 Adrienne LaFrance, "The Six Main Arcs in Storytelling, as Identified by an A.I.," *The Atlantic*, July 12, 2016, https://www.theatlantic.com/technology/archive/2016/07/the-six-main-arcs-in-storytelling-identified-by-a-computer/490733.

85 Chris Higgins, "Vonnegut's Letter to His Family About His Imprisonment in Slaughterhouse Five," *Mental Floss*, January 13, 2010, https://www.mentalfloss.com/article/23699/vonneguts-letter-his-family-about-his-imprisonment-slaughterhouse-five.

86 Stuart Miller, "Inside Otis Redding's Final Masterpiece '(Sittin' on) the Dock of the Bay'," *Rolling Stone*, December 10, 2017, https://www.rollingstone.com/music/music-features/inside-otis-reddings-final-masterpiece-sittin-on-the-dock-of-the-bay-122170.

87 Sally Jenkins, "Why Are Jim Thorpe's Olympic Records Still Not Recognized?," *Smithsonian Magazine*, July 2012, https://www.smithsonianmag.com/history/why-are-jim-thorpes-olympic-records-still-not-recognized-130986336.

88 Lucinda Hawksley, "How did A Christmas Carol Come to Be?," *BBC*, December 22, 2017, http://www.bbc.com/culture/story/20171215-how-did-a-christmas-carol-come-to-be.

89 Clive Francis, "Ten things you never knew about Charles Dickens's A Christmas Carol," *The Telegraph*, December 5, 2012, https://www.telegraph.co.uk/culture/charles-dickens/9724579/Ten-things-you-never-knew-about-Charles-Dickenss-A-Christmas-Carol.html.

90 John Byrne, *The Whiz Kids: The Founding Fathers of American Business* (New York: Doubleday Business, 1993).

91 Charles Cooley, *Human Nature and the Social Order* (New York: Cornell University Library, 1902).

92 Elizabeth R. Thornton, *Objective Leader: How to Leverage the Power of Seeing Things As They Are* (New York: Palgrave Macmillan, 2015), 97.

93 Trevor Haynes, "Dopamine, Smartphones & You: A battle for your time," *Harvard University Blog*, May 1, 2018, http://sitn.hms.harvard.edu/flash/2018/dopamine-smartphones-battle-time.

94 Andrea Nagy Smith, "What was Polaroid thinking?," *Yale Insights*, November 4, 2009, https://insights.som.yale.edu/insights/what-was-polaroid-thinking.

95 Springs Toledo, "A Birthday for Sonny Liston," *The Sweet Science*, September 1, 2012, https://tss.ib.tv/boxing/featured-boxing-articles-boxing-news-videos-rankings-and-results/15175-a-birthday-for-sonny-liston.

96 Aaron Hicklin, "David Bowie: An Obituary," *The Sweet Science*, January 11, 2016, https://www.out.com/music/2016/1/11/david-bowie-obituary.

97 Molly Guptill Manning, "A Tree Grows in Guadalcanal: How a Novel by Betty Smith Brought Comfort to Battle-Weary Soldiers During WWII," *HuffPost*, December 6, 2017, https://www.huffpost.com/entry/world-war-book-brooklyn_b_6257550.

98 Molly Guptill Manning, *When Books Went to War: The Stories That Helped Us Win World War II* (New York: First Mariner Books, 2014).

99 Guptill Manning, "A Tree Grows in Guadalcanal."

100 Jack London, *Martin Eden*, (New York: Penguin Books, 1993).

101 Joseph McAleer, *Call of the Atlantic: Jack London's Publishing Odyssey Overseas, 1902-1916*, (Oxford: Oxford University Press, 2016), 73.

102 Gwen Thompkins, "Forebears: Bessie Smith, The Empress Of The Blues," *NPR*, January 5, 2018, https://www.npr.org/2018/01/05/575422226/forebears-bessie-smith-the-empress-of-the-blues.

103 Carman Moore, "Blues and Bessie Smith," *The New York Times*, March 9, 1969, pp. 262, 270.